THE MAKING OF SHEFFIELD

'THE MAKING OF ...' Series

The Making of ...' series is a new collection of local histories, brought to you by Wharncliffe Books. This series is not intended to be a chronological account of each area, but instead highlights the prominent factors, which bring to life the development and character of a town, city or area. These highly illustrated books contain illuminating snapshots captivating the history and growth of each locality.

'ASPECTS' Series

With over 32 books currently available in Series, *'Aspects'* books are unique in that they allow many local authors and historians to contribute articles to each volume. Articles are made up from a collection of nostalgic and historical pieces relevant to an area, each of which is highly illustrated.

'FOUL DEEDS AND SUSPICIOUS DEATHS' Series

Each book will take the reader into the darker side of their town or region; covering stories that once shocked, horrified and captivated the people who lived there. From the strange to the macabre, to murder and mystery, the authors examine those cases, analysing both motive and consequence, alongside the social conditions prevalent at the time.

Please contact us via any of the methods below for more information or a catalogue.

WHARNCLIFFE BOOKS
47 Church Street • Barnsley • South Yorkshire • S70 2AS
Tel: 01226 734555 • 734222   Fax: 01226 734438
E-mail: enquiries@pen-and-sword.co.uk • **Website:** www.pen-and-sword.co.uk

The Making of
SHEFFIELD

Melvyn Jones

Series Editor
Brian Elliott

Wharncliffe Books

First Published in Great Britain in 2004 by
Wharncliffe Local History
an imprint of
Pen and Sword Books Ltd.
47 Church Street
Barnsley
South Yorkshire
S70 2AS

Copyright © Melvyn Jones, 2004

ISBN: 1-903425-42-5

Typeset in 10/12pt Plantin by Mac Style Ltd, Scarborough.

Printed and bound in England by
CPI UK.

Pen and Sword Books Ltd incorporates the Imprints of
Pen & Sword Aviation, Pen & Sword Maritime,
Pen & Sword Military, Wharncliffe Local History,
Pen & Sword Select, Pen and Sword Military Classica
and Leo Cooper.

For a complete list of Pen & Sword titles please contact
PEN & SWORD BOOKS LIMITED
47 Church Street
Barnsley
South Yorkshire
S70 2BR
England
E-mail: enquiries@pen-and-sword.co.uk
Website: www.pen-and-sword.co.uk

Cover Illustration: *From a painting by Gerry Kersey*

Contents

A jobbing grinder at the Globe Works in the 1970s working in almost Dickensian conditions. Peter Machan

$\mathcal{I}$NTRODUCTION

T he **Making of Sheffield** has not been an easy book to write, not because of having to search hard for material to include but because of the problem of what to leave out and when to stop – 40,000 words and 100+ illustrations seems a high mountain to climb in the early days of writing, but eventually it becomes a matter of cruel editing as whole chapters and dozens of little seen or original illustrations are discarded. And I have been only too aware of my illustrious forbears in this endeavour: Hunter, Gatty, Leader, Stainton (who wrote a book with exactly the same title as this, published in 1924), Walton, Tweedale and Hey, to name just a few who have written with flair and originality on the subject.

The end result is a history not just of the original parish and its six constituent townships that formed the original borough and then city but also including the former parts of Derbyshire and the old West Riding incorporated into the city at various dates. Covering thousands of years and a multitude of topics *The Making of Sheffield* tells the story of the development from a group of small agricultural settlements into a town and then a modern city. It covers successes, disappointments, miserable periods and glorious episodes that have marked the city's evolution – the creation of a busy market town beneath and beside the walls of its medieval castle, the development of a magnificent deer park, the Earl of Shrewsbury's role as gaoler of Mary Queen of Scots in the castle and Manor Lodge, the cholera epidemic of 1832, the rise and fall of Sheffield as cutlery capital of the world, Sheffield city of steel, and Sheffield in its Edwardian pomp. The book not only uncovers what happened and when, it celebrates many of the people who shaped the city or brought attention to it because it was their birthplace, from the Norman lords de Lovetot and de Furnival, the Earls of Shrewsbury, inventors such as Benjamin Huntsman, Thomas Boulsover and James Vickers, cutlers such as George Wostenholm and John Rodgers, heavy steel manufacturers such as Sir John Brown, Mark Firth and Sir Robert Hadfield and scientists, engineers and architects such as Harry Brearley, Henry Clifton Sorby, Sir John Fowler and William Flockton, to literary and artistic talents such as Ebenezer Elliott, Sir Francis Chantrey and members of the Gatty family.

The book could not have been produced without the help of a number of key organisations and individuals. First, I would like to thank Brian Elliott, Series Editor, for inviting me to write this volume and for his subsequent help and encouragement. Secondly, I would like to thank Mrs C J Durdy and Mr Geoffrey Woodcock for allowing me to use material from family diaries and journals in their possession, Bob Warburton for a number of maps and drawings, and Gerry Kersey for the cover illustration. I would also like to acknowledge the assistance of members of staff in Sheffield Archives and Sheffield Local Studies Library over a long number of years. Last and not least, I would like to thank my wife Joan for proof reading, for her many helpful suggestions, her photographs and her forbearance.

A Peopled Landscape: The Area Before the Establishment of the Norman Town of Sheffield

The physical setting of Sheffield is equalled by no other British city. It is enveloped in the west by very extensive tracts of high moorland and upland pasture rising to nearly 550 metres (more than 1800 feet), all within the modern city boundaries. From this lofty surround a large number of rivers and streams, not only the Don and its five major tributaries, the Little Don, the Loxley, the Rivelin, the Porter and the Sheaf, but a myriad of minor brooks and becks such as Ewden Beck, Blackburn Brook, Limb Brook, Moss Brook and Wyming Brook have cut their courses, leaving deep valleys, many still wooded and semi-rural in their western and southern upper and middle courses. Even further east there are deep valleys, as in the Sheaf valley at Beauchief, and prominent edges and hills, as at Brincliffe Edge and Wincobank Hill. Beside the River Rother in the far south-east at Beighton the land is no more than 40

A nineteenth century engraving of Stanedge. Sheffield and Neighbourhood, Pawson & Brailsford, 1889

metres (about 130 feet) above sea level. The modern metropolitan area is built on a series of escarpments and hills and in the intervening valleys.

The first inhabitants: hunter-gatherers of the Palaeolithic

Before 10,000 BC this dramatic landscape was roamed by a small population of hunter-gatherers, the Palaeolithic (Old Stone Age) people whose shelters were crudely constructed of timber and skins or in caves and whose tools and weapons were of stone or bone. They survived by hunting the 'big game' that lived in the area – animals such as bison, horse and red deer in the warmest periods of forest vegetation and mammoth, woolly rhinoceros and reindeer when the climate deteriorated and tundra conditions prevailed with only moss, lichens, coarse grass and low, stunted bushes to sustain the animal populations. In the severest climatic periods, sometimes lasting for tens of thousands of years the ground was permanently below moving ice sheets and the human population left the area altogether, only to move northwards again as climatic conditions ameliorated. The human population of the local area in the Palaeolithic period would have been very small with each small group developing a cycle of seasonal movements over a well-known territory following the herds of animals they hunted. Ice movement and the associated scouring of the landscape have removed a great deal of archaeological evidence but Palaeolithic tools and weapons have been found to the east and south-east of Sheffield in the river gravels of the Trent valley and in Deadman's Cave in Anston Stones wood on the Magnesian Limestone east of Rotherham and more importantly in the caves at Creswell Crags in North Derbyshire.

Hunter-fisher-gatherers of the post-glacial woodlands

Rising temperatures 12,000 years ago resulted in the melting and shrinking of the most recent glaciers and ice sheets which led to a rise in sea levels, and by about 6,000 BC, in the creation of Great Britain as an island separated from the continent of Europe. The rising temperatures also resulted in the thawing of frozen ground and, most importantly, in a gradual change in the vegetation culminating, by about 7,000 BC in a more or less continuous tree cover as species moved in on the wind and in the droppings of birds and animals from those parts of Europe that had lain beyond the grip of ice and freezing conditions to form the primaeval forest called by woodland historians the 'wildwood'.[1]

Two interesting glimpses of the fully developed wildwood in the local area come from pollen analysis and the remains of fallen trees subsequently buried below peat deposits. Conway (1947) and Hicks (1971) made studies of pollen on the moorlands in the western part of the city and suggested that by 4,000 BC the area was covered by a mixed oak forest with the canopy broken by areas of damp heath and swampy areas with alder and birch.[2] More recent studies in the Humberhead Levels to the east of Doncaster using the evidence of both pollen analysis and buried trees have suggested that before the drowning of the wildwood there, between 3,500 and 2,500 BC, there was on Thorne Moors a mixture of marshy woodland in the wettest areas made up of birch, willow and alder, deciduous woodland dominated by oak on the clay-silts and native pine forest on the sands. On the sands and gravels of nearby Hatfield Moors the wildwood consisted of native pine woodland with oak locally present and patches of more open heathland.[3]

Pollen analysis suggests that there were permanent glades of varying sizes scattered throughout the wildwood which would have been grazed and kept relatively treeless by wild cattle, swine and red deer.

As the environment changed from tundra to forest after 10,000 BC the surviving human population gradually began to subsist on smaller prey (mammals, fish and birds) of forest, marsh, river and lake and the more abundant fruit, nuts and roots. Mammals included wild cattle, red deer, horse, wild pig, bear and beaver. The bow and arrow had been invented by this time and it was perfectly fitted for silent and patient hunting in a forest environment.

The impact of these hunter-fisher-gatherers, known as the Mesolithic (Middle Stone Age) peoples, on the natural environment, like their predecessors, would have been negligible. All they have left behind in the Sheffield area are their tools and weapons. Finds have been made on the gritstone moorlands to the west of the built-up area of Sheffield where they have been preserved beneath peat deposits and then revealed as the peat has eroded. Finds have been rarer further east because of disturbance by later cultures and burying under residential and industrial developments, but important finds have been made at Bradfield, Deepcar and Wincobank within Sheffield and at Hooton Roberts and Canklow in Rotherham. At Deepcar, for example, what appears to have been a temporary camp beside the River Don, where flint tools had been prepared, yielded more than 23,000 artefacts (including debris from working flints). There were signs of a shelter, possibly a windbreak, around three hearths. Thousands of Mesolithic tools and weapons from Bradfield and Hooton Roberts were collected by 'field walking'

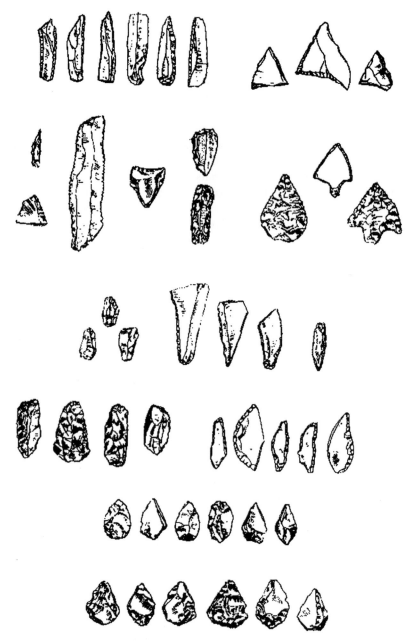

Mesolithic flint tools and weapons collected by Reginald Gatty in Bradfield and Hooton Roberts. Reliquary and Illustrated Archaeologist, January, 1900

by Reginald Gatty, the Rector of both places between 1869–1888 (Bradfield) and 1888–1914 (Hooton Roberts). As described by himself his technique was on a spring morning 'to enter the farmer's gate and follow the toiling horses. It is not long before a ray of sunlight flashes on a flint flake, and I stoop, and capture my prize'.[4] Part of his collection is in Weston Park Museum in Sheffield and Clifton Park Museum in Rotherham.

The most characteristic artefact of the late Mesolithic period is the microlith, i.e., a very small worked stone, most commonly flint or chert (flint-like quartz). A microlith is either in the shape of a very small arrowhead or a barb, and these would have normally been fitted into a wooden shaft to make a multi-faceted arrow, harpoon or spear suitable for hunting.

In the late Mesolithic period hunting became more intensive and the forest environment appears in some places to have been managed by felling and burning the wildwood to entice deer into areas of new, highly palatable growth. This development foreshadowed the later domestication of pigs, sheep, goats and cattle.

The first permanent settlers and farmers
While the Mesolithic peoples of the Sheffield area were following their hunting-fishing-gathering lifestyle a revolution was taking place in the Middle East and Mediterranean Europe. This was the development of agriculture from about 8,000 BC accompanied by pottery making and weaving. This agricultural revolution involved the domestication of pigs, sheep, goats and cattle, the breeding of horses, the invention of ploughing and the growing of cereals, and the eventual change from a semi-nomadic existence to one where settlement sites were occupied on a more or less permanent basis.

These innovations spread throughout Europe through farmers colonising new lands and hunter-gathers adopting them through contact with farming communities and they reached the British Isles between 3,000–4,000 BC. Colonists must have introduced cereals and sheep because these are not native to Britain. At first farmers and hunter-gatherers must have lived side by side but by about 3,000 BC pastoral farming had replaced hunter-gathering as the main means of subsistence in the southern Pennine and sub-Pennine areas This was the beginning of what is called the Neolithic (New Stone) Age. But despite the 'Neolithic Revolution' tools were still of stone, although finished more expertly and the wide range of igneous and metamorphic rocks employed suggest strongly that they were often acquired through long-distance trading. Unlike neighbouring

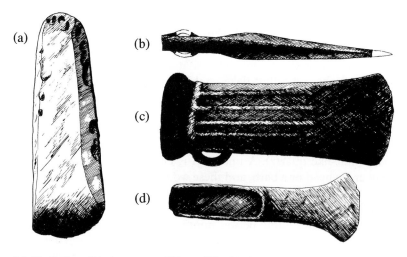

(a) Neolithic polished stone axe, Wharncliffe; (b) Bronze spearhead, Stannington; (c) Bronze axe, Wybourn estate; (d) Bronze palstave, Rivelin valley.

Derbyshire no Neolithic settlements or sacred monuments have been found in the Sheffield area, and the presence of this culture in the area is only known from the chance finds of tools and weapons.

A series of later farming cultures succeeded the Neolithic in the rest of the prehistoric period and beyond into the succeeding period of Roman rule. The Bronze Age which succeeded the Neolithic probably began in the Sheffield area about 1650 BC. Although stone continued to be used for tool and weapon manufacture, this culture marked the beginning of the use of smelted metals. Bronze is an alloy made by smelting copper with tin. Finds of bronze tools from this period include axes, daggers, spearheads and decorative pins recovered from burial cairns on the Millstone Grit moors or as chance finds. Other features associated with the Bronze Age include stone circles associated with burial, for example on Broomhead, Burbage and Totley Moors, a few funerary urns and rocks with cup-shape hollows and incised circles called cup and ring markings.

The Bronze Age was succeeded in South Yorkshire by the Iron Age about 700 BC. Smelted iron tools took the place of those made of bronze but this is likely to have been a slow process, distant as the area was from the centre of technological progress in the south of England. The major archaeological feature of the Iron Age still surviving in the present landscape is the fort. Each fort would have been surrounded by a farmed countryside whose inhabitants would

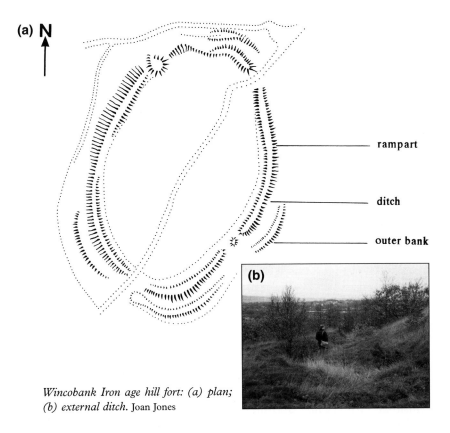

*Wincobank Iron age hill fort: (a) plan;
(b) external ditch.* Joan Jones

have owed allegiance to a local chieftain and would have looked
towards the fort for protection in times of unrest. Seven and possibly
eight such forts survive in South Yorkshire, two of them (Wincobank
and Carl Wark, although some doubt still exists about the dating of
the latter) within Sheffield City boundaries and the site of a third
which formerly existed in Roe Wood is well known.

The Wincobank hill fort occupies a commanding position
overlooking the lower Don valley near the present day boundary
between Sheffield and Rotherham. It lies only at 160 metres (525
feet) but as the land slopes away steeply in all directions its presence
is felt for several miles around. Wincobank Hill is a hog's back (a long
narrow hill) of Coal Measures sandstone bounded on the north-east
by the valley of the Blackburn Brook and on the south-west by a
minor stream at Grimesthorpe. The result is a dry, easily defended
hilltop with good views all around. Today the grass-covered rampart
at Wincobank is more or less complete but the ditch and outer bank

are absent along most of the western side of the fort and along the northern part of the eastern side. Excavations by Sheffield City Museums in 1899 and 1979 have shown that the rampart was originally made as a stone wall several metres thick bonded together by timbers. The stone rampart would almost certainly have been topped by a palisade. When the rampart was excavated it was found that the timbers had been burned, suggesting that the fort was destroyed by fire. The charcoal from the burnt timbers gave a carbon date suggesting that the trees had been felled to construct the fort about 500 BC.[5]

During the succeeding Roman period (AD 43–410) the area within the modern Sheffield City boundaries was not occupied by the Romans and the nearest Romans were found in the Peak District to the south, and at the fort at Templeborough just beyond the Sheffield boundary in Rotherham, first established as a timber fort in AD 54 and rebuilt in stone about AD 100. During the Roman period the local British population would have been engaged in farming activities, slow population growth would have taken place, settlement would have continued to spread and there would have been considerable impact on the wildwood as new sites were occupied for cereal growing, then abandoned and kept as open woodland because of the pressure of grazing animals. Minor earthwork enclosures and field systems of the Iron Age and the succeeding Romano-British period are features of hilltops and plateaus in the lower parts of the Millstone Grit country and the neighbouring Coal Measures in the

Wharncliffe: (a) the dramatic crags (b) a beehive quern. Drawing by Bob Warburton

Sheffield area, the best known being on the escarpment between Wharncliffe and Grenoside.[6]

The growing intensity of cereal growing can be gauged from the fact that it gave rise in the Iron Age and Roman period to a quern making industry in the Loxley and Rivelin valleys and at Wharncliffe. Querns were hand-operated grindstones for making flour from cereal grains. The site at Wharncliffe is at the foot of the crags just inside the Sheffield boundary and covers 72 hectares (178 acres). Thousands of 'flat-disc' and 'beehive' querns in various stages of production still survive on site. It is thought that the 'factory' may have had its origins in the Bronze Age and that it was still active in the medieval period with its main phases of production in the Iron Age and Roman period.[7]

Anglo-Saxon and Viking colonisation: the place-names legacy
Some way down Wincobank Hill from the Iron Age hill fort is the remnant of another earthwork called the Roman Ridge or Rig. This is a linear earthwork in the form of a bank or bank and ditch which stretches with breaks for almost sixteen kilometres (ten miles) along the northern side of the Don valley as far as Mexborough. In one stretch it is in the form of two banks more than 800 metres apart. Despite its name it is not thought to be Roman, although dating the feature remains a problem. It was long thought to be prehistoric, and possibly built at the same time as the hill fort at Wincobank. It has also been suggested that it is of 'Dark Age' origin, built sometime between AD 410 and AD 600 after the collapse of the Roman Empire, possibly to defend the Celtic kingdom of Elmet (which stretched from Leeds to Sheffield) from the advancing Anglo-Saxons.[8]

The Anglo-Saxons were colonists who settled the lowland parts of eastern and southern Britain after the departure of the Romans in *c* AD 410. They were Germanic tribespeople who came from the coastlands of north-western Europe, from the lower reaches of the River Rhine to the River Elbe and southern Jutland. The Anglo-Saxon settlers in the Sheffield area, who were mainly Angles from southern Jutland, entered a land that had been peopled for many thousands of years and had been farmed for than 3,500 years. It was several centuries after the Anglo-Saxon settlement took place in the fifth century in eastern and south-eastern England before they penetrated into the Sheffield area, probably no earlier than the early seventh century. Within another century and a half they were joined by another group of colonists from the continent – Danish Vikings.

The Viking age is said to have begun in 793 when the monastery of Lindisfarne was plundered. Raiding of the Yorkshire coast took place in the first half of the ninth century and in 865 a Danish army conquered a large part of eastern and north-eastern England. The growing Danish population was short of agricultural land and the Danish war leaders were followed by agricultural settlers and the Sheffield area became part of Danelaw. Again, as in the case of the Anglo-Saxon settlers before them, the Danish agriculturists settled in gaps in the existing settlement pattern, often on second-best sites. The Danish settlers were joined in the West Riding in the tenth century by Norwegian settlers who had moved from Ireland into western Britain and then moved eastwards onto land unoccupied on the eastern side of the Pennines.

Although archaeologically, the Sheffield area is poor in Anglo-Saxon and Viking remains, it is very rich in Anglo-Saxon and Viking place-names. The name of the city, almost every district name, almost all the village names within the city boundaries and most of the names of individual farms and even the old names of fields and lanes and some city streets can be traced back to Old English or Old Norse origins, the languages spoken by the Anglo-Saxons and Vikings respectively. Old English and Old Norse vocabulary relating to settlements continued to be used in the medieval period but because there are few documentary records of Sheffield area names before 1086 when the Domesday Book was written it is not possible to say exactly how ancient local names are. But etymological studies (i.e. studies of the formation of a word and its meaning) have been able to ascribe probable much earlier origins to names that are first recorded in the eleventh century and later.[9]

This is of course certain to be true of names believed to be of Celtic or pre-Celtic origin or which refer to a Celtic population already living in the area when the later Anglo-Saxon settlers arrived. For example, the name of Sheffield's major river, the Don, which also appears in Russia and forms the first part of the river name Danube is now believed to be of pre-Celtic origin.[10] That a Celtic population existed in South Yorkshire when the Anglo-Saxons arrived is testified by a few Anglo-Saxon place-names that have survived referring to the Celtic population and their settlements. For example, the Old English *walh* means foreigner, Briton or Welshman and this has survived in the name of the village of Wales, just eight miles east of Sheffield in Rotherham Metropolitan Borough. Another Celtic word that occurs in two Sheffield place-names is *egles*, which is itself borrowed from the Latin *ecclesia*. It means church and is presumed to refer to the presence of a Christian church being acknowledged by

St Mary's church, Ecclesfield. The church, largely rebuilt between 1480–1520, stands in an elevated position at the western end of the village on the site of a much earlier Christian shrine that gave the village its name. Chapeltown & High Green Archive.

the heathen Anglo-Saxons. The word occurs in the names of Ecclesfield (treeless stretch of country containing a British church) and Ecclesall (nook of land containing a British church).

The purely Anglo-Saxon (Old English) and Danish Viking (Old Norse) place-names in the Sheffield area can be divided into main types: habitative names and topographical names. Habitative names have as their main part (usually second or last and called the suffix) a word meaning settlement such as farm, hamlet, village or town, estate or enclosure. Topographical names have as their suffix a word referring to the physical setting of the place such as hill, valley or woodland clearing. It used to be thought that habitative names were the earliest Anglo-Saxon names but one modern scholar at least has written persuasively that topographical are possibly the earliest names given to places in England by the Anglo-Saxons based on the evidence of places that are known to have been changed from their original topographical names to habitative ones.[11] Unfortunately the paucity of pre-Domesday documentary records for the Sheffield area (they only exist for a few of the places in the south of the city originally in Derbyshire) makes it impossible to test this idea in Sheffield.

Old English place-names
The most common Old English habitative names found in England are *-ham* (homestead), *-tun* (now usually spelt *-ton* and meaning farm, village or estate) and *-worth* (enclosed settlement). There are only two

-*ham* names in the Domesday Book of 1086 in the whole of South Yorkshire, and very few others recorded after that date, none of them in the Sheffield area. This is not surprising as -*ham* was the most commonly used habitative name at the very beginning of the Anglo-Saxon period nearly three centuries before they settled in South Yorkshire. There are four -*tun* names within the present city boundaries: Beighton, Norton, Owlerton and Stannington. The first two, both then in Derbyshire appear in the Domesday Book. Owlerton, which was not recorded for the first time till 1310 means the 'farm near the alders'. There are a few more surviving -*worth* names, five altogether: Dungworth, Handsworth, Hemsworth, Holdworth and Sugworth, together with one lost -*worth*, Hawksworth. The -*worth* names are very often combined with an Anglo-Saxon personal name as in the cases of Holdworth (Halda's enclosure), Hemsworth (Hemele's enclosure) and Hawksworth (Hafoc's enclosure).

The most common Old English topographical name in England is -*leah* meaning a wood or more commonly a woodland clearing, and it is very common within Sheffield occurring on more than a dozen occasions: Birley, Cowley, Hartley, Heeley, Longley, Loxley, Mortomley, Plumbley, Totley, Wadsley, Walkley, Whiteley, Whitley, Woolley and the less obvious Gleadless and Norton Lees. The large number of -*leah* names testify to the well wooded landscape of the area in Saxon and early medieval times – a re-calculation of woodland areas for Sheffield at Domesday show that at that time more than twenty-two per cent of the modern Sheffield Metropolitan District (20,000 acres) was still wooded.[12] As with the habitative names, a number of the local -*leah* names have as their first element an Anglo-Saxon personal name as in Loxley (Locc's clearing), Totley (a corruption of the Domesday entry of *Totingelei* meaning Tota's people's clearing) and Walkley (Walca's clearing). Others are descriptive of the site or of the animals found there as in Heeley (high clearing), Longley (long clearing), Cowley, (clearing where charcoal was made) Hartley (stag clearing), Gleadless (possibly kite (the bird) clearing) and Woolley (wolf clearing). Tinsley is not a -*ley* name at all but a corruption of *Tineslauue* or *Tyneslawe* meaning Tynni's mound.

The element -*feld*, meaning a stretch of treeless country or heath in an otherwise well-wooded area, is also a common Old English topographical place-name element but it only occurs a few times in the Sheffield area: Ecclesfield (already noted above), Ballifield, Hallfield, Bradfield (broad treeless area), and most notably Sheffield (treeless area beside the River Sheaf).

There are also a group of Old English place-names in the Sheffield area that refer to the hilly nature of the landscape and the deep river valleys crossing the area in the west. These include *-clif* (edge or escarpment) as in Brincliffe (probably edge cleared by burning), Yarncliffe in the Mayfield valley (eagle cliff or edge), Shirecliffe (bright steep hillside) and Wharncliffe meaning quern-cliff as already noted above. Waldershelf above Stocksbridge includes the element *-scelf*, meaning shelving terrain, and wooded or previously wooded heights are recalled in the name Herdings (from *Heytridding*) meaning a high clearing in the woods and *-hyrst* (a wooded hill) as in Fair Hurst at Bradfield and Scraith, the earliest spelling of which seems to represent *scraith-hirst* (wood on a steep scree slope). Another interesting place-name element is *-halh*, in modern spelling usually *–all*, meaning a secluded nook of land, sometimes on a hillside sometimes in the far corner of an existing estate. Surviving *–halh* names in the Sheffield area include Ecclesall, already noted, and Darnall and Worrall. It may also be that the first part of the ancient name Hallam (first mentioned in the Domesday Book in 1086) and Hallamshire (first mentioned as such in 1161), the latter being the name for the Norman lordship incorporating Sheffield, Ecclesfield and Bradfield, may also be derived from *halh*, followed by um or am meaning 'at the'.[13] There are also a number of interesting names referring to the area's river valleys as in Midhope and Midhopestones which contain the Old English word *-hop* meaning a small enclosed valley and Agden (oak valley), Dwarriden (dwarf valley), Ewden (yew-tree valley), and Howden (hollow valley) all containing the element *-denu* meaning a long, curving, narrow valley. Finally, the odd-sounding name of Wigtwizzle contains the element *-twisla*, the confluence of two streams, with the full name meaning Wicga's river-fork.

Viking place-names
The Viking place-names come in three forms. Either they are purely (the prefix and the suffix) in Old Norse, dialects of which were spoken by the Danes and Norwegians; or they are a combination of Old Norse and Old English (what are known as hybrid names); or they are Scandinavianised, i.e. the Vikings changed the Old English prefix, suffix, or both into a sound like one in their own language because they could not or preferred not to pronounce the word in the Old English way.

The most common Old Norse place-element in Yorkshire is *–by*. There are 210 *-by* place-names recorded in the Domesday Book in Yorkshire with another 69 first recorded in pre-Domesday documents. When used by the Danes it meant a village or town and when used by

Onesacre. This hamlet with the hybrid name (the prefix is the Old Norse personal name, An, *coupled with the Old English suffix* aecer, *together meaning 'An's plot of cultivated land', was recorded in Domesday Book in 1086.* Joan Jones

the Norwegians it meant a farm. The element is still used today in the word *by-law* meaning a local law. There are ten places in South Yorkshire containing this place-name element but all but one are in the eastern part of the region, with five – Barnby Dun, Scawsby, Balby, Cadeby and Denaby beside the River Don, probably a major colonisation route. None occurs within Sheffield's boundaries.

The second most common Viking place-name element, associated with areas settled by Danes is *-thorp*, which means an outlying farm or hamlet dependent upon a larger settlement, and most rural examples are still only single farms, hamlets or small villages. Including places that have long disappeared or where the Old Norse name has been replaced by another, there are known to have been about thirty *thorps* across South Yorkshire, including a good number within Sheffield's boundaries. Among those still surviving are Grimesthorpe, Upperthorpe, Hackenthorpe, Waterthorpe and Jordanthorpe. Grimesthorpe (Grim's outlying farmstead) is particularly interesting because it seems to have replaced in the medieval period (it is first recorded in 1297) the Domesday place-name of *Grimeshou* (Grim's mound or burial place).Equally interesting is the modernisation of the place-name Upperthorpe, which might be thought to refer to a farmstead near the top of a hill on the south side of the River Don as opposed to nearby Netherthorpe nearer the river below it. Nothing could be more wrong: Upperthorpe first recorded as Hoperthorpp in 1383, has as its first element the Middle English surname Hopere, meaning a barrel-maker or cooper. The initial letter H has been lost, and the much more modern name of Netherthorpe given to the area lower down the slope. There are also three lost *-thorp* names that once occurred in the area to the south of the boundary of Sheffield parish with that of Ecclesfield: Raynaldsthorpe (later changed to Hatfield House Farm), and Osgathorpe and Skinnerthorpe, both of the latter two now only surviving as street names.

The third most common Viking place-name element in South Yorkshire is *-thveit* (*-thwaite*) meaning woodland clearing, but only one example is found within Sheffield's boundaries – Butterthwaite in Ecclesfield, which means woodland clearing with rich pasture. Among other Scandinavian names in the Sheffield area are a few wholly Scandinavianised names and one or two hybrid names (part Old English and part Old Norse). For example, *lundr* in Lound Side at Chapeltown is an Old Norse name for a wood, as is *storth* in the hamlet name of Storrs to the west of Stannington; and Onesacre, meaning An's plot of cultivated land and Ughill (Ugga's hill), both of which were recorded in the Domseday Book, have Old Norse prefixes (personal names) and Old English suffixes. Another interesting hybrid name is Grenoside, made up of three elements, the Old English *graefen* meaning a quarry, the Old Norse *haugr* meaning hill, and the relatively modern addition of the word *side* giving *graefen-haugr-side*, (quarried-hill-side), Grenoside.

In addition to these town, village, hamlet and farm names there are the names of fields and lanes and other minor features that show that Old Norse was once widely used throughout the area. *Kjarr* (marsh) for example, which survives in the hybrid name Carbrook (stream in the marsh) but was once much more widespread as a field name. The use of *eng*, usually spelt as *ing* was also widespread in river valleys and means damp meadow land and it occurs on a number of occasions in John Harrison's survey of the Manor of Sheffield in 1637 as in Barbat Ing, Lathe Inge and Owler Inge.[14] The Old Norse word *gata*, now spelt 'gate', meaning lane or street, is a Viking word now usually associated with urban areas – Barnsley has its Eastgate and Westgate, Rotherham has its Bridgegate, Doncaster Gate, Moorgate and Wellgate, and Doncaster has even more including the evocative Baxter Gate (street of the bakers). Sheffield only has one, Fargate, which was not recorded until about 1700. It should also be noted that the word gate was also introduced to the mining industry at an early date for the name of the main underground roadway (the main gate) in a colliery.

Finally, the Vikings also gave a number of old administrative divisions in South Yorkshire. Sheffield was of course for centuries part of the old West Riding of Yorkshire 'riding' being the old Viking name

Butterthwaite, a hamlet in Ecclesfield parish first recorded in the thirteenth century. The name means 'clearing (Old Norse thveit*) with rich pasture* (butere).
Chapeltown & High Green Archive

(*thrithungr*) for a third part. At a more local level the Viking word *bierlow* (Old Norse *byar-log*) was in the past attached to the names of Brightside and Ecclesall in Sheffield parish and to the four sub-divisions of Bradfield (Bradfield, Dungworth, Waldershelf and Westnall). 'Bierlow' means the law of the village, and when attached to the name of a community simply meant a small locality in which local laws had been enacted to deal with minor disputes.

The Sheffield area at the beginning of the Norman period

When the Norman lords and their retinues entered South Yorkshire shortly after their success at the Battle of Hastings in 1066, they were entering an area that was heavily settled and peopled. We know this from the Domesday survey conducted twenty years later in 1086 by William the Conqueror to find out about ownership of the land before and after the Conquest and to determine the value of each property (called a manor). Although there are some notable omissions, what the Domesday survey did was to record many places for the very first time. In what was to become the parish of Sheffield, Sheffield and Hallam (recorded as *Hallun*), Attercliffe and Darnall were recorded for the first time, as was *Grimeshou*, later changed to

Grimesthorpe. In neighbouring Ecclesfield parish, besides Ecclesfield itself, the Domesday Book also recorded Holdworth above the Loxley valley, Ughill to the west of Stannington, and Worrall and what today is the tiny hamlet of Onesacre, both in the upper Don valley. But sixteen berewicks (dependent small settlements within a manor) in Sheffield manor, which were said to exist in the survey were tantalisingly left unnamed. So there was no mention of villages such as Bradfield, Grenoside, Heeley or Stannington, for example, and documentary records do not mention these places until one century (Bradfield) or even two centuries later, even though they had probably been in existence for hundreds of years at the time of the Domesday survey. Other places beyond Hallamshire but now within the city boundaries were recorded in the Domesday survey. These include Tinsley, which was incorporated into Sheffield in 1921, and the villages formerly in Derbyshire: Beighton, Mosborough, Norton, Totley, and Dore, the latter name being recorded as early as 828. Until their dramatic collapse under attacks from the Danes in 865 and 873 respectively, Dore stood on the boundary between the Anglo-Saxon kingdoms of Northumbria to the north (in which Hallamshire lay) and Mercia to the south, and the name means a narrow pass from which we get the modern name 'door'.

The Normans who controlled the country for three centuries after the Conquest of 1066, brought a new language to South Yorkshire, Norman-French. This became the language of power, control and ownership.[15] The de Lovetots built and the de Furnivals re-built a castle (from the Old French (OF) *chastel*) at the confluence of the Don and Sheaf from where they ruled their Hallamshire estate (OF *estat*) through baliliffs (OF *baillif*) and their regular manorial courts (OF *cort*) through which they dispensed justice (OF *justice*). They also established a park (OF *parc*) from which they procured their venison (OF *veneson*) to accompany their beef (OF *boef*), pork (OF *porc*) and mutton (OF *mouton*) at their banquets (OF *banquets*).

They also gave to the English town and countryside a new vocabulary of place-names. Well-known ones in various parts of the country include Grosmont in North Yorkshire, maeaning 'big hill', Egremont in Cumbria meaning 'sharp-pointed hill' and Pontefract in West Yorkshire meaning 'broken bridge'. They also prefixed a substantial number of names with beau or bel meaning 'beautiful' or 'fine' as in the case of Belvoir in Leicestershire (beautiful view) or Beaulieu in Hampshire (beautiful place) and, of course, one of the few Norman-French names in the Sheffield area, Beauchief, meaning 'beautiful headland', referring to the beautiful wooded spur which rises behind the abbey, and incidentally sharing the same Norman-French name as Beachy Head. There are very few other Old French place-names in the Sheffield area. There is parc in Park Hill, of course; rocher (rocks) referring to the steep rocky hillsides at Rocher, Rocher End, Rocher Flat and Rocher Head to the north of Bradfield; and Waterthorpe at Mosborough which was not recorded for the first time till 1376 and has as its prefix not an Anglo-Saxon or a Viking personal name but a Norman one, Walter.[16] The same is true of Jordan in Jordanthorpe, not recorded until 1296. Both of these possibly late -thorp names suggest the continued use of this Viking word for an outlying farm was still in use locally hundreds of years after the Vikings first colonised the area.

Beside their castle the Norman manorial lords of Hallamshire created the town of Sheffield and the character of the early town and its surrounding countryside is discussed in the next chapter.

Beauchief Abbey, showing on the right the foot of the bold wooded escarpment that prompted the monks who founded the abbey in 1176 to call the place Beauchief *(beautiful headland)*. Samuel Pegge, An Historical Account of Beauchief Abbey, 1801

2 $\mathcal{T}$HE EARLY TOWN OF SHEFFIELD AND ITS SURROUNDING COUNTRYSIDE

The early town

Sheffield began life as a town rather than a village under its Norman lords. The Norman town was established immediately to the south-west of the confluence of the rivers Don and Sheaf where, in the twelfth century, William de Lovetot built a motte and bailey castle with a stone and timber keep, possibly on a site continuously occupied since at least the Iron Age. Excavations carried out on the castle site in the 1920s found not only the remains of a timber-framed Saxon building but also Roman pottery. The two rivers formed a natural moat to the Norman castle on the north and east. This motte and bailey castle which had descended to the de Furnival family at the end of the twelfth century was destroyed by fire in the second half of the thirteenth century during the baron's revolt and was replaced by Thomas de Furnival with a stone keep and bailey castle about 1270. This stone castle was largely demolished in the late 1640s by Cromwell's government following the Civil War when it was garrisoned for the King until it surrendered in 1644. Following its demolition it was plundered by the local population for building stone and other buildings occupied the site. For these reasons precise details of its layout have not survived. The excavations carried out in the late 1920s, when the Brightside and Carbrook Co-operative Society was building new business premises on the corner of Waingate and Exchange Street and Sheffield Corporation commenced building work on the Castle Market site, revealed stretches of stone wall, a circular bastion next to the main gateway, possibly part of the gatehouse and its drawbridge support and many interesting medieval artefacts in what had been the moat.[1]

John Harrison in his survey of the manor of Sheffield in 1637 said the castle was 'fairely built with stone & very spacious'. It comprised an inner courtyard bounded on the west and south by a moat which Harrison called a 'great ditch', and with 'ye Great River of Doun lying on ye north parte thereof & ye Lesser River called ye Little Sheath on ye east'. To the south of the moat was an outer courtyard which Harrison said contained an armoury, a granary, barns, stables and 'divers Lodgeings'.[2] At its greatest extent this outer bailey is thought to have run south from the moat up the slope as far as the modern Fitzalan Square. Thomas Winder, who worked for many

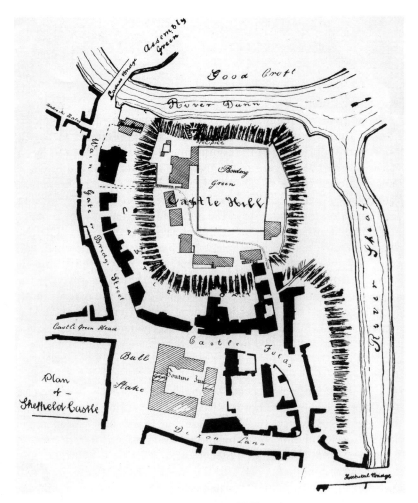

Thomas Winder's sketch map of the site of Sheffield castle.

years in the Duke of Norfolk's estate office in Sheffield, put together
a sketch map of the castle site based on old maps he had consulted.
The map shows a square hill on which the keep was located, the moat
south and east between the Don and Sheaf, and the close relationship
between the keep and the entry into the town across the River Don
via Lady's Bridge.

The medieval market town of Sheffield grew up under the
protection of the castle. In 1281 Thomas de Furnival was asked by a
royal enquiry into the rights of landowners (called *Quo Warranto* – by

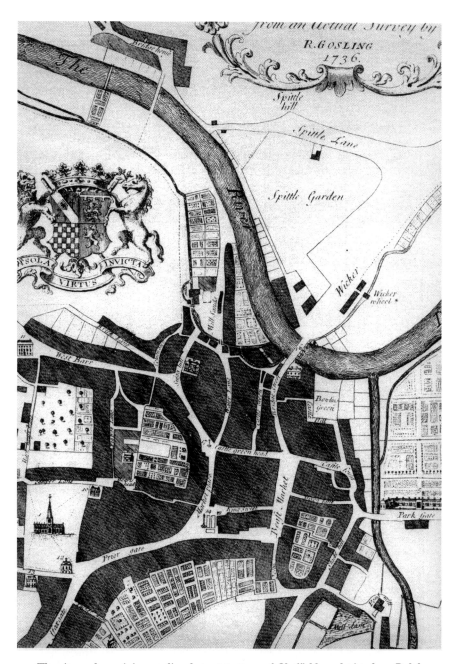

The site and surviving medieval street pattern of Sheffield as depicted on Ralph Gosling's map of 1736.

what right), on what grounds he believed he had the right to hold a market in Sheffield, and he replied that his ancestors had held it since the Norman Conquest. He put this right to hold a market on a more formal footing fifteen years later when in 1296 he obtained a royal charter for a market every Tuesday and a fair at the Feast of Holy Trinity which fell in either May or June.

Beneath the castle walls in a tight cluster of narrow streets including what is the modern Market Place, Haymarket (formerly called the Beast Market and before that the Bull Stake), Waingate (formerly called Bridge Street), Castle Green, Castle Folds, Dixon Lane, Snig Hill, and the now lost Pudding Lane, Water Lane and Truelove's Gutter (which was also an open sewer) lay the oldest part of the town which had probably first emerged at the same time as

Surviving timber-framed buildings in Snig Hill at the end of the nineteenth century. Harold Rodgers

William de Lovetots's motte and bailey castle. Surviving documents from the late sixteenth century give the impression, 500 years after its first creation, of a tightly-knit collection of houses, cottages and shops with their outbuildings, gardens, crofts and yards. A rental of 1581, for example, contains descriptions such as 'a cottage with ii bayes newe erected and builded this yere', 'a house and smethie', 'a cottage at Sheff. Park yate beneath ye Castell' and 'a house and backsyde over and against Thomas Horner'. Intermingled among the buildings were pig styes ('swyne hulls'), small paddocks ('foldes', 'closes' and 'intacks'), gardens and places for piling manure ('myddensteds').[3]

Before the seventeenth century all the houses in the town would have been timber-framed. A detailed set of accounts have survived relating to the building of a new house for William Dickenson, the agent for the Earl of Shrewsbury's Sheffield estate.[4] The accounts give details of sixteen trees that were purchased and payments that were made for 'posting' the timber (i.e., squaring and preparing joints in the main timber components), 'leading' the posts and beams from the wood to the house site, 'rearing' the house (i.e., lifting and securing the timber framework in position) and 'Dawbinge' (i.e., covering with a mixture of straw and clay the panels between the vertical timber posts which would have been filled with wattle or very thin stone slates). On the day the house was reared Dickenson spent the relatively large amount of 48 shillings and 8 pence on celebrating the occasion.

The central area immediately to the south-west of the castle was the town's main retail area. The rental of 1581 itemises eight shops under and around 'ye Court Chamber' which was another name for a market hall with a room at first floor level but open underneath. The 1581 rental also describes four 'payntesses' and 'stannedges' near the courthouse. A payntess was a pentice, a shed attached to a building and stannedge was probably a 'standing', so these appear to have been market stalls probably with wooden shutters that could be opened upwards to form a protective awning and downwards to form a display counter. In 1581 one of the stalls was held by a fishmonger and three by tanners selling leather which was used in a wide variety of ways, not only for boots and shoes but also for harnesses, saddles, breeches, aprons, gloves and mittens, bellows, bags and bottles. Nearby were twelve butchers' shops, two of them said to be new and three of them in the 'shamblehowse', the meat market. Here too was the market cross and the Bull Stake where the town bull may have been tethered for hire. In nearby Pudding Lane, a narrow lane between the Market Place and the Bull Stake (Beast Market), was the public bakehouse, where, as late as 1609 one of the 'paynes' (by-laws) agreed by a jury at the manorial court stated that all the householders within the town of Sheffield should bake their bread there.

From this central core beneath the castle walls, the town spread out in all directions. To the east along what became known as Dixon Lane the way led to the River Sheaf where a stone bridge was built in 1596 and which led to the castle orchards, on the southern edge of which in 1666, fifty years after his death, Gilbert, 7th Earl of Shrewsbury's Hospital was erected for the housing of twenty-four poor townsfolk. To the south-west the town spread along what is the modern High Street but what until the late eighteenth century was known as Prior

Long, narrow burgage plots, sometimes separated by narrow lanes on the south side of Fargate as shown on the 1921 25 inch OS map of central Sheffield (Yorkshire Sheet 294.08).

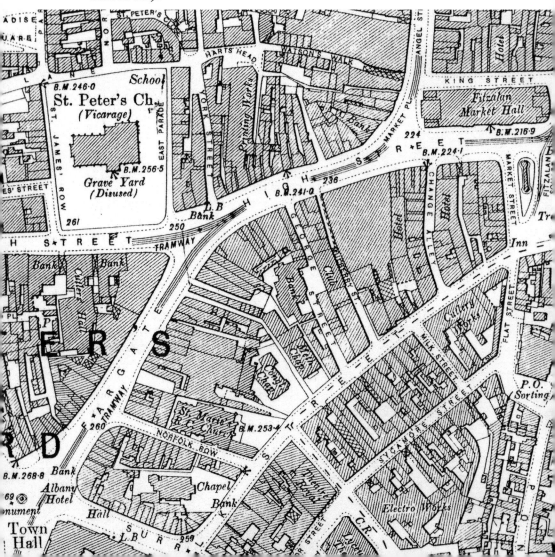

The tomb of George Talbot, 4th Earl of Shrewsbury in Sheffield Cathedral. Joan Jones

Gate because it contained properties belonging to Worksop Priory that had provided a vicar for the church in return for one-third of Sheffield's tithes. Beyond High Street was a lane that became known as Fargate (gate (*gata*) being the Danish Viking word for a lane). Along both sides of High Street and the southern side of Fargate today can still be seen the evidence of the late medieval and early modern expansion of the town in the form of long narrow building plots sometimes separated by long alleys such as Change Alley, Mulberry Street and Chapel Walk. The long building plots, called burgess plots because they were occupied by the citizens (burgesses) of the town, reflect the desire to allow as many shop, workshop and other workplace owners to have a commercial frontage on a main street.

At the junction of High street and Church Street at the south-eastern corner of the churchyard, stood the early town hall, the meeting place for the twelve Capital Burgesses, a body of men set up in 1554 by the 5th Earl of Shrewsbury to regulate the town's affairs. To the north of this was the medieval parish church, now the cathedral. By the 1590s this contained the tombs of George 4th Earl of Shrewsbury (1468–1538) and his two wives, and George 6th Earl (*c.*1528–90). On the south side of Church Street, stood the Cutlers' Hall, the headquarters from 1638 of the Cutlers' Company of Hallamshire, formed in 1624 to regulate and organise the cutlery industry in succession to the manorial court. This building was replaced by the present Cutlers' Hall in 1832.

Beyond the far end of Fargate was Balm Green, to the east of the present City Hall, which contained Barker's Pool, a source of fresh water for the town's residents to supplement the supply from public and private wells. Details of major improvements to Barker's Pool survive from 1572. In that year payments were made to William Wornall for walling Barker's Pool, to William Dykar for 'feying' (i.e., cleaning) it, to Robet Greenwood for supplying a bolt and lock and to Thomas Creswyke for a shuttle.[5] The shuttle (a sluice gate) would have been an important feature when water from the pool was occasionally released and channelled through the town to clean its streets, eventually finding its way down Water Lane and Truelove's Gutter into the River Don.

Northwards from the central core, at the bottom end of the Market Place beyond the Irish Cross (which denoted a place where non-natives could sell their goods), was Snig Hill. The probable meaning of the word 'snig' is for a block of wood that was put through cart wheels to act as a brake, and as Snig Hill led to the town's manorial corn mill at Millsands, many a heavy load must have had to be braked on the steep hill. At the bottom of Snig Hill was West Bar, a name possibly denoting a gate into the early town, but this must remain a presumption as no other town entrance has survived as a local place name. At West Bar from 1628 stood the town's workhouse.

Lastly, the town extended across the River Don via the stone-built Lady's Bridge, constructed in 1486 to replace an earlier timber structure. This late medieval bridge which is hidden below the modern bridge stood the test of time and attests to the excellent craftsmanship of its builder, master mason William Hyll, and to the critical eye of local citizens. Hyll's instructions in his agreement for building the structure was that he should 'make a suffycient brigge over the watyr of Dune neghe the castell of Sheffield, wele and suffyciently after the sight of workmen of the same crafte and gode men of the parysh'.[6] Lady's Bridge is so-called from the Chapel of Our Blessed Lady of the Bridge which stood to the south of the river under the castle walls. This chantry chapel, where travellers could pray for a safe journey, became disused after the Reformation and had become a wool warehouse by 1572 and later became an almshouse for four poor people. It was rebuilt using stone from the demolished castle after the Civil War. North of Lady's Bridge the road lay across Sembly Green and the Wicker, leading to Spital Hill where William de Lovetot had founded a hospital (hence the name 'spital') outside the town in the twelfth century. On Sembly Green every Easter Tuesday, in the late medieval and early modern period, the lord of the manor or his representative inspected the town's militia consisting in 1637 of about 140 men with 'Horse & Harnesse' for 'Confirmeing of the Peace of our Sovereigne Lord the King'.[7] On the Wicker were the town's archery butts and, until it was removed to Barker's Pool, a 'cucking-stool' for ducking women who spread malicious gossip and other objectionable persons! In 1572 payments were made to workmen for 'making of the cook stoole', and for irons, locks and staples for it.[8] Whether this was a new cucking-stool replacing a former one that had fallen to pieces through regular use will never be known!

As has already been hinted at, the water-power of Sheffield's rivers was harnessed for industry at an early date and by 1637 rent was being paid to the lord of the manor for at least nine water-powered corn mills and twenty-nine cutlers' wheels. Forges and furnaces were also in operation.

Throughout the medieval period and into the early modern period Sheffield was not only a small market town with a developing industrial hinterland but also the headquarters for a large surrounding country estate. Intermingled with the rented farms, cottages, water-powered mills and quarries were two areas that remained under the direct supervision and management of the lord of the manor's officials. These were Rivelin Chase and Sheffield deer park.

Rivelin Chase
Rivelin Chase was the generic name for a group of private forests of the lords of the manor of Sheffield. Forest in this case does not signify an area covered by trees, indeed large parts of Rivelin Chase were moorland, but one in which a private version of the Royal Forest Law applied relating to the grazing and hunting of deer and other game, which were regarded as the private property of the lord of the manor; the grazing of farm animals; the felling of timber; and the clearing of land. Forests did not have boundary fences and were intermingled with settlements and farms. Rivelin Chase included at its fullest extent not only Rivelin Chase proper, but also the Forest of Fulwood and Loxley Chase and a number of smaller areas under Forest Law called 'firths', e.g., Grenofirth. At its fullest extent Rivelin Chase

extended westwards from the confluence of the Loxley and Rivelin at Malin Bridge covering most of the township of Upper Hallam and large parts of Bradfield parish. In 1637, for example, in John Harrison's survey of the manor of Sheffield, 'Rivelin ffirth that lyeth in the parish of Sheffield' was said to cover more than 5,500 acres; he also recorded 1,114 acres of Rivelin Firth in Bradfield parish, together with Stannington Wood which was also said to be part of the Chase and which covered 217 acres. Other firths that were recorded in 1637 but not specifically recorded as part of Rivelin Firth were Loxley Wood and 'ffirth' which covered 1,517 acres and Hawkesworth 'ffirth' which covered nearly 8,000 acres.[9] In an account of the 4th Earl of Shrewsbury's foresters in 1441–42 the Pennine valleys of Agden, Yewden, Howden and Harden are also mentioned.[10]

The hunting of deer and other game for sport or for the table – Harrison in 1637 mentioned that the manor of Sheffield was furnished 'for pleasure' with red, fallow and roe deer, hares, pheasants, partridges, black and red grouse, moorhens, mallard, teal, heron (which he called 'hearnshews') and plovers[11] – was only an occasional pursuit of the lord and his guests and his professional foresters, and income was earned by allowing pasturage of animals

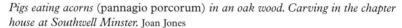

Pigs eating acorns (pannagio porcorum) *in an oak wood. Carving in the chapter house at Southwell Minster.* Joan Jones

and exploitation of other natural resources and the collection of fines from those who broke the Forest Law. In the 1441–42 account, for example, the forester for 'Bradfeld' recorded income (or lack of it) for pasturage (other records specifically mention cattle and sheep being pastured), pannage of pigs, (*de pannagio porcorum*), the sale of branch- and brushwood (*ramayllis*) (from which Sheffielders get the word 'rammel' now meaning rubbish) and the sale of holly for winter feed for animals (*De hussis ... pro brousingys animaliun tempore yemali...*). In the same account the forester for 'Ryvelynge' recorded pasturing rents for plough cattle, and income from sales of wood and timber and brushwood and for grinding wheels (presumably quarried) from the lord's quarry. But the forester also recorded that there was no income in that year from wood sold for charcoal making, from road tolls, from the sale of roof slates from the quarry, for pannage of pigs (because no mast (*pessona*), ie, acorns had fallen from the trees that year) and no fines had been exacted from fishermen fishing in the streams. The forester of 'Granowe' (Greno) recorded income from the grass of the pasture in Beeley Wood (*Bylleywode*) and for the lease of a coal pit.

The Old Laund in Rivelin Chase as it might have been depicted on a sixteenth century map.

Although Rivelin Firth contained thousands of acres of moorland, there were also important woodlands and ancient wooded pasture with 'veteran' oak trees, particularly in the Rivelin valley. John Evelyn, writing in his book *Silva*, first published in 1669, said that Rivelin, apart from Hawe Park, was by then 'destitute' of its mighty oaks, but he described one that had recently been felled, called the 'Lord's Oak' which was twelve yards (i.e., 36 feet or 11 metres) in circumference.[12] In the 1630s John Harrison described an important landscape feature within Rivelin Chase that had become characteristic of a wooded forest or deer park. This was an area largely devoid of trees with a rich crop of grass and herbs where the deer came to feed and which could be enclosed by a paling fence or wall and in which culling could take place. The glade was called by the Norman-French name, *laund*, from which we get the modern word lawn. Harrison described Rivelin laund, which was located on rising land to the north of the river and extended to 62 acres, as 'ye Old Laund reserved for ye Deare being Invironed by Rivelin Firth'.[13]

The illegal hunting of game and the illegal felling and carrying away of wood and timber in Rivelin Chase must have been relatively common occurrences and it was the foresters' duty to bring offenders before the manorial court. For example, in 1385 Thomas Horsknave was fined threepence for cutting wood in Grenofirth[14]; in 1564 Thomas Beaumont was fined twelvepence for felling and taking away two loads of wood from 'le Firth of Revelinge'[15]; and in 1595 in a letter to the 7th Earl of Shrewsbury it was reported that 'Edward Bromhall and his man have been taken for supposed hunting in Locksley'.[16]

Sheffield deer park
Much nearer to the medieval and early modern town was the lord of the manor's deer park. The deer park, which at its greatest extent

Sheffield deer park, 2,462 acres (nearly 1000 hectares) in size and eight miles (eleven kilometres) in circumference. The named areas are those mentioned in John Harrison's survey of the manor of Sheffield in 1637. At that date the park contained 1,000 fallow deer.

covered 2,462 acres (nearly 1,000 hectares) and was eight miles (13 kilometres) in circumference came right up to the eastern edge of the town. It had a typical shape, a rounded rectangle which was the most economic shape for fencing. The boundary fence, called the park pale, in the case of Sheffield deer park, appears to have been, in the late medieval period at least, a high cleft-oak paling fence. We know this from a record of 1441–42, which states that a payment was paid to John Legge and John Gotsone for repairing defects in the rails and paling around the park.[17] The park had three functions: to keep the deer in and to keep poachers and predators out. And it was not only the deer that were in danger; besides the deer, a deer park often held hares, rabbits (in the medieval period often in artificially made burrows in so-called 'pillow mounds'), wild boar, fish in specially made fish ponds and a variety of game birds. Deer parks also contained valuable timber resources. The temptation was often too much for certain sections of the population and at the court leet of the manor of Sheffield in 1578 six local men were each fined five shillings 'for huntinge the hare within my Lordes Parke ... to the disrurbance of my Lordes game there, & killed one deare & dyd hyte an other deare'.[18]

It cannot be stressed enough that the function of a deer park was not primarily for hunting for pleasure, but as a status symbol and to provide the owner with a regular supply of food for the table and supplies of wood and timber. For example, for the great dinner held in Sheffield Castle following the funeral of the 5th Earl of Shrewsbury in 1560, fifty does (female fallow deer) and twenty-nine red deer had been killed and cooked.[19] Because all deer were said to belong to the king, from the beginning of the thirteenth century it was necessary to obtain a Royal licence to create a deer park and to kill deer, called a right of free warren. These were issued to princes, lords, knights, archbishops and bishops and they were also attached to monasteries, nunneries and colleges. The fish ponds in the deer park attached to Beauchief Abbey still survive and further afield Magdelene College, Oxford, still has its deer park full of deer in the middle of the town! Ecclesall Woods stand on the site of a deer park (the top part of the wood is still called Park Head) created following the granting of a right of free warren to Sir Robert de Ecclesall in 1319, and another deer park, called Shirecliffe Park, once stood on the northern slopes of the middle Don valley where the settlement of Parkwood Springs grew up, following the granting of a right of free warren to Sir John de Mounteney in 1392.[20] The creation of Sheffield deer park predates the issuing of rights of free warren and so must have been of eleventh or twelfth century origin at least – possibly it was created in the late Saxon period. Thomas de Furnival, lord of the manor of Sheffield, when asked to explain before the *Quo Warranto* enquiry of 1281 by what right he held Sheffield deer park, said his family had held it (like the right to hold a market) since the Norman Conquest of 1066.

By the seventeenth century the park was in decline but still contained a number of very important features. By 1637 when John Harrison carried out his survey of the manor of Sheffield more than 971 acres (more than a third of the park) had been let to tenants, including the whole of the northern part of the park, called the Little Park, all that part of the Great Park to the west of the Sheaf, and all but two enclosures amounting to 80 acres in the western third of the Great Park to the east of the Sheaf.[21] The tenanted parts of the park in 1637 were a mixture of arable, grazing and meadow land, and also included a coppice wood on Morton Bank. They also included Heeley Side which was grazing land in which there were coal pits which Harrison said 'yieldeth great profit unto the Lord'. These coal pits were mentioned as early as 1441–42.

Those parts of the park still managed as a deer park in 1637, contained 1,000 fallow deer, including 200 antlered bucks, or as Harrison put it 'Deare of Auntler'. Harrison named the various parts of the park including some with woodland names including Arbor Thorn Hirst and Stone Hirst (hirst was the name for a wooded hill) but they would only have been covered with scrub woods of hawthorn and holly. Holly was important fodder for deer and cattle and in the 1441–42 accounts for the park there are several references to the cropping of holly trees. Other names

Fallow deer grazing beneath an ancient oak, a scene that would have been a familiar one in Sheffield deer park from early medieval times until sometime in the seventeenth century. The Author

mentioned by Harrison such as ye Lands, Cundit Plaine, Blacko Plaine and Bellhouse Plaine suggest grazing areas with scattered trees. Ye Lands is probably a corruption of the Norman-French word *laund*, already referred to in Rivelin Chase, and the word plain has a similar meaning. The launds and plains would certainly have contained a scattering of trees, some of them pollarded above the height of grazing animals, and many of a great size and age. Some of these trees were described in great detail by John Evelyn in his book *Silva*. He appears to have obtained his information from Edmund Morphy, one of the Duke of Norfolk's woodwards. Evelyn described one oak tree in the park whose trunk was thirteen feet in diameter and another which was ten yards in circumference. On Conduit Plain (the Cundit Plaine of Harrison's 1637 survey), Evelyn reported that there was one oak tree whose boughs were so far spreading that he estimated (giving all his calculations) that 251 horses could stand in its shade. He also described another massive oak that when cut down yielded 1,400 'wairs' which were planks two yards long and one yard wide and 20 'cords' (more than forty tons of four foot lengths of wood) from its branches. Finally, he described another oak, that when felled and lying on its side was so massive that two men on horseback on either side of it could not see each other's hat crowns![22]

There were two important buildings standing in the park by the beginning of the sixteenth century. In the north-western corner, beside the ponds which eventually formed the water power for a second lord of the manor's corn mill, stood the Hall in the Ponds. Dendrochronological (tree-ring) analysis shows that this timber-framed building, which survives in part today as the *Old Queen's Head* public house, was built of timber felled between 1503–1510.[23] The building is jettied on the south, west and east sides, has close-studded walls, a king post roof and carved heads on the exterior of the ground-floor posts. The two-storeyed building originally had a single two-bayed room on each floor, with the first floor room open to the roof. In an inventory of its contents compiled in 1582 the building was said to contain 'peces of paynted hangings' and window and chimney pieces of canvas, a trestle table, two 'buffet formes', a 'buffet stoule', a still, a flagon, pewter dishes and a spit, all suggesting it was used for the preparation of meals and dining in a very comfortable setting.[24] It may originally have been a banqueting house for the lord of the manor and his guests at the end of a day's hunting, fishing and fowling in the park. Significantly, in a letter from an estate official in Sheffield to the 7th Earl of Shrewsbury and his Countess in 1599

The Hall in the Ponds as depicted in Hunter's Hallamshire (1819). The building still survives as the Old Queen's Head *public house.*

(who were in London) an account is given of stocking with fish 'the Pond mill dam' for the Earl's use.[25]

On a much larger scale than the Hall in the Ponds, was the Manor Lodge, located near the centre of the park with glorious views in all directions. This was originally a hunting lodge, converted into a comfortable country residence by George, the 4th Earl of Shrewsbury. Harrison in his survey of 1637 described it as 'being fairly built with stone & Timber with an Inward & an outward Court 2 Gardens & 3 Yards'.[26] Mostly in ruins now, only the Turret House near the entrance to the site still survives largely intact. On the second floor of the Turret House is a room with an original Elizabethan fireplace and decorated plaster ceiling. The Manor Lodge is famous because Mary, Queen of Scots, spent much time here during her long imprisonment under George, 6th Earl of Shrewsbury. This is the subject of the next chapter.

The Manor Lodge as depicted in an early nineteenth century engraving.

'*T*HE CUSTODY OF THE SCOTCH QUEEN': MARY, QUEEN OF SCOTS, IN CAPTIVITY IN SHEFFIELD

3

Sometime during the morning on 28 November 1570 a large party mounted on horseback, perhaps numbering a hundred or more, began to make its way northwards on a twelve-mile journey from Chatsworth House in North Derbyshire across the moorlands into South Yorkshire and the town of Sheffield. The riders reached the southern outskirts of the town in mid-afternoon and made their way without pomp – although no doubt looked upon in curiosity and awe by villagers and townsfolk – to its northern extremity, where, almost circled by the rivers Don and Sheaf, stood the stone-built castle. Once inside the inner courtyard, while the rest of the party remained on horseback, one of the male riders assisted a female rider to dismount and led her into the hall and to her private apartments. George Talbot, the 6th Earl of Shrewsbury, had safely delivered Mary, Queen of Scots, to his Sheffield stronghold. She was to remain in captivity in Sheffield for almost fourteen years.

For perhaps the only time in its history, during those fourteen years Sheffield would have been constantly on the lips and in the minds of the court and government in London. She spent nearly a third of her life here yet in most history books the details of Mary, Queen of Scots' captivity in Sheffield are given little space. For example, in Antonia

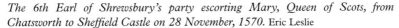

The 6th Earl of Shrewsbury's party escorting Mary, Queen of Scots, from Chatsworth to Sheffield Castle on 28 November, 1570. Eric Leslie

Fraser's *Mary Queen of Scots* (1969)[1], domestic details of Mary's captivity in Sheffield are covered in only a few of the 568 pages and in Professor Gordon Donaldson's *Mary Queen of Scots* (1974)[2], only twenty-two pages (out of 194) are devoted to Mary's captivity in England and even in those pages the Earl of Shrewsbury and Sheffield receive only the briefest of mentions. The same is true of the latest life of Mary, *My Heart is My Own* by Professor John Guy (2004).[3] Fortunately, Sheffield's own historians in the nineteenth century more than made up the gap. Joseph Hunter in his monumental *History of Hallamshire* first published in 1819 and revised and extended in 1869 and 1875[4] began by saying that 'little has been said of the occurrences which passed while she was immured in Shrewsbury's strong castle of Sheffield'. He went on to say that neither had any attempt been made to 'give a connected view of her private history during the long period of her captivity'.[5] He followed this over the next twelve pages by giving a year by year summary of that history.[6] The editor and reviser of the 1869 and 1875 editions of the *History of Hallamshire*, Dr Alfred Gatty, vicar of Ecclesfield, also wrote pieces about Mary's captivity in Sheffield for the younger generation. In 1871 he wrote an article in *Aunt Judy's Magazine* entitled 'The Captivity of Mary, Queen of Scots'.[7] The magazine, which was edited by the author's wife, Margaret Gatty, had a world-wide readership. At one point in the article Gatty commented that historians had generally ignored the period of her captivity in the town and that as a result 'Sheffield had been excluded from a fair place in the page of history'. Four years later, in 1875, Gatty published his history for the 'rising generation' of the town, *Sheffield: Past and Present*.[8] In that volume he wrote a long and detailed chapter about Mary's period of captivity in Sheffield, which he began by stating that 'No poet, novelist or playwright ever conceived a tale comparable in sad interest'. But the most significant local contribution appeared in 1880 with the publication of John Daniel Leader's exhaustive (it covers 642 pages) *Mary Queen of Scots in Captivity: a Narrative of Events*.[9] In his Preface he states that he was emboldened to write about Mary, Queen of Scots, 'that well-worn subject' because he intended to write about that part of her life 'which has least occupied the attention of historians and biographers'. Leader had access to much previously unpublished material in the Public Record Office. Much more recently, Keith Cheetham, formerly Sheffield's conference and tourist officer has written two interesting accounts of Mary's life.[10]

Keen-eyed city residents and visitors can still see a few signs of Mary's long stay in Sheffield. In the Transport Exchange (ie, the bus

The Old Queen's Head *public house.* Joan Jones

station) is the public house called the *Old Queen's Head* once probably a banqueting house in the deer park (see Chapter 2) and reputedly a place she visited while in Sheffield, although there is no direct evidence for this belief. There is also a modern public house which bears her name - the *Scottish Queen* on South Street on Park Hill within the former territory of the deer park where she was held at various times in the Manor Lodge. Finally, in the Chapter House of Sheffield Cathedral there is a series of stained glass windows depicting the history of Sheffield and the surrounding area by Christopher Webb (born 1866). One of these windows shows Mary sitting in front of a fireplace in the Turret House at the Manor Lodge with her secretary, Pierre Rollet. Rollet died while Mary was in captivity in Sheffield and he is buried in the Cathedral churchyard. Beside Mary's chair is a piece of embroidery she has been working on.

Mary and her secretary, Pierre Rollett, in a stained-glass window in the chapter house of Sheffield Cathedral. Courtesy of the Provost and Chapter of Sheffield Cathedral.

Mary's life prior to her exile in England

Mary, Queen of Scots, the only surviving legitimate child of King
James V of Scotland and Mary of Guise, a French noblewoman, was
born on 8 December 1542. On 14 December her father, the king,
died, and so at the age of only six days, Mary became Queen of
Scotland.

As a small child Mary's destiny was contested by England and
France. Henry VIII proposed that Mary should marry his son
Edward, so that eventually the English and Scottish thrones would be
united. Mary's French uncles, on the other hand, proposed that Mary
should marry Francis, heir to Henry II of France. The French
marriage was favoured and Mary was sent to the French court as a
six-year old (Francis was four). She spent the whole of her childhood
there, French was her first language, and a Regent (her mother) took
her place in Scotland.

In April 1558, when she was still fifteen, she was married to the
fourteen year-old Francis at Notre Dame Cathedral in Paris. Later in
the same year, Queen Mary Tudor of England, who had succeeded
Edward VI (for whom Mary, Queen of Scots had been considered as
a queen while still an infant), died and Henry II of France advanced
her case to be the next queen of England ahead of Elizabeth. This
claim was based on the fact that Mary was a direct descendant of the
English royal family (her grandmother was Henry VIII's sister) while
from the Catholic standpoint Elizabeth was illegitimate (Elizabeth's
mother, Ann Boleyn became Henry VIII's wife only after his divorce
(not recognised by the Pope) of Catherine of Aragon.

In July 1559 Henry II died from wounds inflicted while jousting
and Mary found herself queen consort of France to King Francis II.
This situation was short-lived however. In December 1560 Francis
died, was succeeded by his younger brother Charles, and Mary
prepared to return to Scotland. Mary returned to a Scotland that had
undergone a religious Reformation, so she found herself a Roman
Catholic queen of a largely Protestant country. She also proclaimed
herself the rightful queen of England. In the first five years of her
Scottish rule, by a combination of personality and tolerant policies
she gained the support of many politically influential men and
popular approval among her Scottish subjects.

But there was still the question of whom she ought to marry:
alliances had to be cemented and an heir produced. Many suitors
were proposed but in the end Mary chose Henry, Lord Darnley, her
first cousin, and another possible heir to the English throne (his
grandmother, Margaret Tudor, was the sister of Henry VIII). He was

Mary, Queen of Scots, as a young woman.

nineteen and described as 'more like a woman than a man, for he was handsome, beardless and baby-faced'. They were married in July 1565. High expectations and infatuation on Mary's part were quickly dissipated when it became clear that Darnley was an immature and dissolute consort, more interested in hunting, hawking, music and women than in government. Moreover, he was a jealous husband. On her marriage to Darnley, Mary had become distanced from her most loyal advisor, the Earl of Moray, and replaced him as her confidant and advisor with her Italian secretary, David Rizzio. On 9 March 1566, Darnley and a group of conspirators, who were as much interested in destabilising Mary's reign as in exacting vengeance on Darnley's perceived rival (who was also suspected of adultery with Mary), entered the Queen's apartments (Mary was then heavily pregnant with the future James VI of Scotland/James I of England), Rizzio was dragged outside and brutally stabbed to death.

Following Rizzio's murder, and the birth of her son James in June 1566, Mary came under the influence of the Earl of Bothwell, a sophisticated, much-travelled adventurer, who had accompanied her from France in 1561. In January 1567, when Mary was pregnant by Bothwell, Darnley was murdered in mysterious circumstances – the house in Edinburgh in which he was staying was blown up, but his body was found outside without any external signs of injury. Bothwell was implicated in the murder and eight years later on his deathbed in a Danish prison where he was being held for piracy, he is reputed to have written (but only copies exist) a confession to the murder of Darnley while proclaiming that Mary was innocent of the crime.

Three months after Darnley's murder Mary married Bothwell. This third marriage sealed Mary's fate. Her subjects were scandalised: they began to believe she had been part of the plot to kill

Darnley; and in some quarters it was concluded that there could never be stability while she remained on the throne. In June 1567 Mary was seized by a group of nobles and imprisoned in Lochleven Castle where she gave birth to still-born twins on 24 July. She was forced to sign a deed of abdication in favour of her infant son, James, and he was crowned King James VI of Scotland on 29 July with the Earl of Moray as Regent.

Mary remained at Lochleven Castle for almost a year before escaping in May 1568. In a desperate attempt to regain her throne she and her followers engaged the army of the Regent but were heavily defeated. She retreated to Dumfries and then sailed in a fishing boat on 16 May across the Solway Firth to Workington, and exile in England.

Exile and captivity in England
Once in England Mary threw herself on the mercy of Queen Elizabeth. This put Elizabeth in a quandary. To allow Mary to remain in England meant that a claimant to the English throne was at large to plot and conspire; to escort her out of the country to France might reinvigorate a Franco-Scottish alliance; to send her to Spain might spark off a European Protestant-Catholic war; and to support her claim for re-instatement as Scottish queen was likely to result in renewed political instability in Scotland. After an inconclusive trial concerning her involvement in Darnley's murder, Mary was held captive in England for eighteen years while Elizabeth pondered a resolution to the problem. The two queens never met.

After a short stay at Carlisle Castle, where in a letter written on 15 June it was related that she had watched a football match between her retainers in which they played 'very strongly, nimbly, and skilfully,

without any foul play'.[11] This is probably the first recorded attendance by royalty at a football match! Mary was then moved to Bolton Castle in Wensleydale. Then, in January 1569, she was escorted to Tutbury Castle in Staffordshire and into the hands of George Talbot, 6th Earl of Shrewsbury. Elizabeth must have seen Shrewsbury as an ideal custodian for Mary. He was rich which was an absolute requirement as he only received

George Talbot, 6th Earl of Shrewsbury.

Bess of Hardwick.

an allowance of £52 per week (which was later reduced to £30), he was powerful and his devotion to Elizabeth was beyond question. Moreover, he and his second wife, the formidable and ambitious Bess of Hardwick, owned vast estates, mostly off the main highways, within which stood fortified and other substantial houses: including Tutbury in Staffordshire; Chatsworth, Hardwick and Wingfield Manor in Derbyshire; Worksop Manor in Nottinghamshire; and Sheffield Castle and the Manor Lodge in South Yorkshire.

Tutbury Castle, a medieval castle leased from the Crown as a hunting lodge proved to be an unsuitable place in which to detain Mary. Although it was easily defended, it was difficult to provision because of its location, and the building was cold and leaked. Mary described her jail as being 'exposed to all the winds and the inclemencies of heaven' and having no drains to the privies 'is subject to a continual stench'. The garden where she was allowed to exercise was no better, being described by Mary as 'fitter to keep pigs in than to bear the name of a garden'.[12] By the end of April 1569 the Earl had moved Mary to more comfortable accommodation at Wingfield Manor where she stayed for six months. During this period a plot was hatched that she should marry the Duke of Norfolk and be restored to the Scottish throne. Elizabeth would have none of it. Norfolk was imprisoned in the Tower of London and Mary was taken back to Tutbury Castle under closer supervision. In mid-November the Catholic Earls of Northumberland and Westmorland marched south bent on rescuing Mary and she was rapidly taken to the walled city of Coventry.

By the beginning of 1570 Mary was back at Tutbury, where she stayed until the end of May, when she was taken to Chatsworth. Mary continued to pass and receive messages and to conspire with the Duke of Norfolk and King Philip of Spain; a plot by members of the Derbyshire gentry to release Mary was uncovered; and a treaty to restore Mary to the Scottish throne was drafted and then eventually dropped by Elizabeth. On the 28 November she was taken to Sheffield.

The proximity of Sheffield Castle and the Manor Lodge was one reason for Mary's long residence in Sheffield. Given the lack of sanitation, houses had to be vacated from time to time for cleaning purposes, and the close proximity of the two houses (less than three miles apart) was very convenient. The Manor Lodge stood in the middle of a deer park eight miles in circumference which ensured privacy plus opportunities for supervised outdoor recreation. The fact that the Earl of Shrewsbury was the major landowner for miles around and could be well informed of comings and goings in the neighbourhood, and that Sheffield was well off major highways were also great advantages.

The regime in Sheffield at the beginning of Mary's detention there was strict. Her retinue was reduced to thirty, none of her attendants could be with her after nine at night nor leave their sleeping quarters before six in the morning; and her servants, with the exception of her Master of the household, were not to wear swords and none was allowed to leave the castle without the Earl's permission. Mary herself had to give one hour's notice to the Earl before leaving her private apartments, and then she was only allowed to walk on the leads of the Castle, in the dining chamber or in the castle yard, in the latter case only in the company of the Earl or the Countess.

Outwardly forbidding, cold and probably damp and draughty, the Castle was not without its comforts. An inventory of 1582 of the Castle and Lodge lists a large number of wall hangings including 'Forrest worke', 'ye storye of Hercules', and 'the storye of the

The Turret House, Manor Lodge. Joan Jones

Passion'. There were also various chimney hangings and eight long and more than a dozen short 'Turkey carpetts'. The window curtains were of taffeta, silk, satin and buckram and the coverings, curtains and counterpanes of the tester beds were of crimson and purple velvet, satin and silk embroidered with silver and gold.[13]

The Earl took into his employ 40 extra servants, selected from among his loyal tenantry, who kept watch day and night at the castle. Still Mary continued to plot her escape and her replacement of Elizabeth as Queen of England, but Shrewsbury's vigilance unearthed several batches of letters in code either being smuggled out of the castle or attempting to be brought into it, in one case inside a hollow staff. Between 1570 and early 1572 the 'Ridolfi' plot brewed. The plot involved a proposed invasion of England by a Spanish army from the Netherlands under the Duke of Alva supported by English Catholic sympathisers under the leadership of the Duke of Norfolk. Queen Elizabeth was to be imprisoned, the Roman Catholic faith be re-instated, and Mary would become Queen of England with the Duke of Norfolk as her consort. Roberto Ridolfi, an Italian merchant banker resident in London who conducted business for and was an advisor to the English government, acted secretly as a go-between with the Pope and the Spanish government as the plot developed. A courier was arrested at Dover, letters were intercepted and the plot discovered. Ridolfi escaped arrest (he was abroad in Europe when the plot was revealed) but the Duke of Norfolk was arrested, imprisoned in the Tower of London and executed in June 1572.

While all this plotting and detection were going on, Mary continued to complain about the conditions of her captivity. In her letters she grumbled repeatedly about being 'without fresh air' and not being allowed the 'necessary exercise'. It was not until 1573 that Mary left the Castle for a stay at the Manor Lodge. By then the Castle must have been in great need of cleaning and airing. But there were concerns at court that the Lodge was vulnerable to anyone determined to secure Mary's release. In a letter to his father, Gilbert Talbot (the Earl's second son, who was to become the 7th Earl of Shrewsbury) reported that he had been approached about this and had told a senior courtier that 'good numbers of men, continually armed, watched her day and night, and both under her windows, over her chamber, and of every side of her; so that, unless she could transform herself to a flea or a mouse, it was impossible that she should escape'.[14] In the event, with the exception of 1576, Mary spent part of every year between 1573 and 1584 at the Lodge.

In the mid-1570s the Earl built at the Manor Lodge what is known as the 'turret house', a small stone-built house with richly decorated ceilings and fireplaces and with access via a small turret to its flat roof. This is the only part of Manor Lodge that survives intact today. In some accounts it is claimed to be a porter's lodge and in others a secure accommodation for Mary. It seems to be very ornately decorated for the former use and is too small for the latter. It may have been a banqueting house built deliberately to take advantage of the fine views over the deer park and beyond, and possibly the prisoner was allowed to take the air there. In May 1582 Mary's coach was sent to Sheffield so that she could be driven in the deer park, but this concession was revoked in September.

Throughout her period of imprisonment, Mary's health was never good and, although at times it was believed she was shamming, it was thought desirable that during the summer she should stay for periods in the country or be taken for a health cure. This also allowed her Sheffield quarters to be thoroughly cleaned (and searched). She went on seven visits to Chatsworth (in 1569 (where she was held immediately before coming to Sheffield), in 1573, 1577 (twice), 1578, 1579 and 1581), two visits to Worksop Manor (both in 1583), but more significantly she also went on six visits of between three weeks and two months to the spa at Buxton to take the waters and use the baths (in 1573, 1574, 1576, 1580, 1582 and 1584). The Earl of Shrewsbury had recently built a house over his well there and this meant that Mary could take the cure in privacy while under close guard. On the first occasion that Mary visited the spa in August 1573

The tomb of George Talbot, 6th Earl of Shrewsbury, in the Shrewsbury Chapel in Sheffield Cathedral. Joan Jones

Shrewsbury was instructed to do it with 'as little foreknowledge abroad as may be conveniently given' and that 'for the time that she shall be there, that all others, being strangers from your Lordship's company, be forbidden to come there...'.[15] The town was in a state of siege for the duration. The same careful precautions seem to have attended all her subsequent visits to the spa.

In between audiences with ambassadors and representatives of Elizabeth's government, Mary was busy with her intrigues and her inveterate letter writing. She also passed the time with her embroideries. In this connection she was continually ordering materials from London or Paris, as in 1574 when she requested her Ambassador in Paris to procure 'patterns of dresses and samples of cloths, gold, silver, and silver strip, the finest and rarest now worn at Court'.[16] He was also to remind one Veratour 'of his promise to send me from Italy the newest kinds of head gear, veils and bands with gold and silver'.[17] On another occasion the French Ambassador was asked to send her 'eight ells of crimson satin, of the colour of the sample of silk I sent you, the best that you can find in London.'.[18] This satin and silk became a 'skirt of crimson satin, worked with silver, very fine' that was delivered by the French Ambassador in a box, sealed with Mary's seal, to Elizabeth. Interestingly, Shrewsbury sent a note with the carrier to the effect that 'Some in my house are infected with the measles, and it may be dangerous for the Queen to receive anything hence before it has been well aired'.[19]

Mary also seemed to be establishing what can only be called a menagerie in her prison quarters. In 1574 she begged her Ambassador in Paris to 'procure me pigeons, red partridges, and hens from Barbary, I intend to endeavour to rear them in this country, or to feed them in cages, as I do all the small birds I can come by - a pastime for a prisoner.'[20] And later the same year she asked her uncle, the Cardinal of Guise, to send her from Lyons a pair of beautiful small dogs ... 'for except reading and working, I take pleasure only in all the little animals I can get'.[21]

Possibly the worst alarm for Shrewsbury during Mary's whole stay in Sheffield, brief though it was, occurred on 26 February 1575 when the castle was shaken by an earth tremor. Shrewsbury wrote to Elizabeth's Secretary of State that on that day 'there came an earthquake which so sunk chiefly her chamber, as I doubted more her falling than her going [ie, escaping]'.[22] Mary herself wrote to the French Ambassador that 'We have had here, even in my chamber, a great earthquake ... insomuch that my women could not sit steady on their boxes and chairs, where they were working round me.'[23]

What must also be remembered is that during the almost fifteen years during which Mary was under the Earl of Shrewsbury's wardenship, he was as much a prisoner as she was and received no visitors except on official business. Queen Elizabeth looked upon any absence of the Earl from direct supervision of Mary as dereliction of duty, and at a very early point in Mary's imprisonment, while she was at Wingfield Manor, the Earl spent three days away at Buxton receiving treatment for his gout without first informing Elizabeth. He received a rebuke for this and had to apologise. Shrewsbury accompanied Mary when she took exercise about the castle and later when she was able to go into the deer park surrounding the Manor Lodge. In his fifteen years as her gaoler, Shrewsbury was only once allowed to go to London - in January 1572 to preside over the trial, for high treason, of the Duke of Norfolk. He was away for less than a month.

Shrewsbury's marriage to Bess of Hardwick was a casualty of his long guardianship of Mary. For the first few years Bess who had been married three times before marrying the Earl of Shrewsbury, shared the burden with the Earl but gradually she began to lead a separate life, busying herself with her affairs as a major landowner, as a builder of houses, and as a champion of her grand-daughter Arabella Stuart as a future queen (Arabella was the daughter of Bess's daughter Elizabeth Cavendish, and married Charles Stuart, Earl of Lennox, whose mother was Mary, Queen of Scots' mother-in-law (mother of the Earl of Darnley). Queen Elizabeth was not pleased when the Cavendish-Stuart marriage took place in late 1574 without her approval, suspecting a plot between the Shrewsburys and Mary. The Earl and the Countess had a big row in 1577 and relations were so bad by 1583 that Bess and her sons were insinuating that Shrewsbury and Mary were lovers. The marriage had broken down completely by 1584. The Earl's health also suffered considerably during his term as Mary's custodian, and he only survived her by just over three years, dying in 1590. Hunter said that marriage to Bess (to whom he is said to have proposed 'in an evil hour') had made the earl 'bitter' and that in later life he was a 'melancholy misanthrope'.[24] Eventually the Earl of Shrewsbury went to live in his house across the deer park in the village Handsworth with the domestic servant, Eleanor Brittain, who became his mistress.

Much to the Earl's relief Mary was moved from Sheffield in 1584. She was soon involved in another conspiracy on this occasion with Anthony Babington, heir to large estates in Derbyshire, who had been a junior member of the Earl of Shrewsbury's household at Sheffield Castle during the early years of Mary's sojourn there. Babington

Mary's execution at Fotheringhay Castle on 8 February, 1587. Drawing based on part of a seventeenth century Dutch painting the original of which is in the Scottish National Portrait Gallery. Mary kneels with her head on the block clutching an ivory crucifix. Beside her are piled her outer garments with her Latin prayer book on top. In the full painting there is a large crowd assembled to witness the execution and through an open door in a courtyard is a fire where her personal belongings are being burned to prevent blood-stained relics of the Roman Catholic martyrdom that she had sought being obtained by her supporters.

acted as messenger between Mary and her friends in 1586 when a Catholic insurrection was planned. Queen Elizabeth and her ministers were to be murdered. Just as the plot was ripening all the conspirators were arrested, tried and hanged. On 8 February 1587 Mary was beheaded at Fotheringhay Castle in Northamptonshire. Ironically, Shrewsbury was involved to the end. As Earl Marshal of England, the premier lord of the realm, he was called upon to issue the order for Mary's execution.

4 $\mathscr{T}$HE CHOLERA EPIDEMIC OF 1832

General background

Sheffield has had its fair share of disasters. For example, the burning of the town and castle during the Barons' Revolt in the thirteenth century with an unknown number of casualties; the great Sheffield flood of 1864 when some 250 people perished; the Blitz of 1940 with 589 deaths, 483 seriously injured and nearly 3,000 houses and shops destroyed or damaged beyond repair; and the Hillsborough football ground disaster of 1989 when ninety-six people were crushed to death at an FA Cup Semi-final. But perhaps worst of all was the cholera epidemic of 1832 because the real cause, and therefore an effective remedy, were unknown; and no one knew if and when the disease would arrive in the town; and once it had struck when the epidemic would end. The cholera epidemic in Sheffield raged for nearly six months and claimed more than 1,350 victims of whom 402 died.[1]

Asiatic Cholera or Cholera Morbus or Spasmodic Cholera, as it was variously called in the early nineteenth century, is endemic in India. In the nineteenth century very severe outbreaks occurred which spread along trade routes by land and sea out of Asia to

The geographical spread of the cholera epidemic that reached England in 1831.

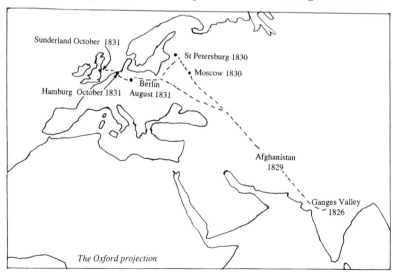

Europe and beyond. In 1817 an outbreak killed 5,000 British soldiers encamped near Calcutta, and the next year the epidemic had engulfed the whole of the Indian subcontinent. There were four major outbreaks which spread to Europe in the nineteenth century one reaching the British Isles in 1831 another in 1848, a third in 1853 and a fourth in 1866.

The 1831 British outbreak began in the Ganges valley in 1826 and quickly spread through the Punjab, through Afghanistan into Persia (modern Iran) in 1829 and then into southern Russia. A letter received in London in November 1830 from the British Ambassador in St Petersburg stated that the 'disorder' then raging in Russia was a 'sort of plague' but the authorities there would not admit it.[2] Russian ships entering British ports were put in quarantine, but this was not very strictly carried out. By August 1831 it had reached Berlin and by October it had spread to Hamburg. It is thought the disease entered Britain at Sunderland on 19 October 1831. By early December more than 350 cases had been reported in Sunderland of which 119 had proved fatal. From there it spread across County Durham, to Scotland where it created havoc in Glasgow and Edinburgh, through the rest of England and Wales to London, and across the Irish Sea to Ireland. By the time it had run its course in the British Isles, 25,000 men, women and children had died in Ireland, 9, 500 in Scotland and 22,000 in England and Wales. The disease went on the medical scale of such things from an epidemic to a pandemic (affecting most of the world). It reached North America in 1832, France, Spain and Portugal in 1833 and Italy and North Africa in 1834. Even Charles Darwin, on his round the world voyage of discovery in *HMS Beagle* was affected. The ship sailed from Devonport on 27 December 1831 and on 6 January 1832 reached Teneriffe. He noted in his journal that they 'were prevented from landing, by fears of our bringing the cholera'.[3]

What must have been particularly unnerving for populations where it struck or for the residents of those centres of population dreading its appearance, was that, as has already been pointed out, although there were strong medical opinions on the matter, there was in the first half of the nineteenth century, no proven explanation for the cause of the disease and no explanation of how and why it subsequently spread from place to place, and therefore there was no adequate cure. Cholera is not contagious, although this is what was thought by many in the 1830s, and therefore isolating patients will not stop it spreading. Joseph Woodcock, a Sheffield brushmaker who lived in Change Alley in the centre of the town, was in his late thirties

The appearance after death of a Sunderland cholera victim. Wellcome Institute

when the epidemic struck. Woodcock kept a journal and devoted 59 foolscap pages to the epidemic.[4] Reflecting much intelligent lay opinion of the time he declared himself an 'infectionist', saying:

> *Indeed I confess myself to be so much of that opinion that from what I have noticed of the disease at Sheffield I would think that there has not been a single case of Cholera in England in either, man, woman or child but what has occurred by Reason of Contact with a Patient labouring under Cholera, or by Reason of Air already contaminated by a Person labouring under the disease.*[5]

The source of the infection, not until 1883 isolated as Koch's Comma Bacillus, must be swallowed to take effect. It was swallowed in contaminated drinking water and was particularly rife where the water supply was from polluted rivers or streams, from springs and from shallow wells, particularly in densely populated urban areas with inadequate sewerage systems which contaminated the streams, rivers, springs and wells.

The occurrence of cholera within a family home must have been a dreadful experience not only for the victims but also for those ministering to them. Woodcock described the symptoms in some detail. He said that a victim of the disease had 'spasmodic Pains in the Bowels, Sickness & Purging and his pulse is scarcely to be felt'. He continued:

> *His eyes look completely sunk and there is a dark circle around them. The Lips are blue or seem as if bloodless, the cold and livid Skin is covered*

with cold, large drops of Perspiration, although sometimes there is a feeling of burning Heat in it. The Hands and feet are not only excessively cold, but are wrinkled, as if they had been held a long time in Water. The Tongue and the Breath are cold.

He went on:

But the Patient also suffers from dreadful spasms, these begin like cramp, in the Feet and Hands and stretch up to the Trunk of the Body – or the muscles of the fore part of the Trunk are violently contracted which is what is meant when it is said that they are affected by Spasms. In some Instances the Spasms are so violent as to render it necessary to hold the Patient down and they sometimes say that they feel as if their Arms and Legs were breaking.

He also described a situation that could aggravate the disease and cause even more rapid decline: 'The Patient feels tormented by heat, throws off the Bed Clothes, & begs of those about him to give him cold Water to drink.' It is, of course, highly likely that if a patient was still at home the drinking water would be contaminated. He also commented succinctly on the rapidity of the fatal impact of cholera: 'A Man is well at Breakfast & dies before Noon.'[6]

Housing and public health in Sheffield in the early 1830s
Sheffield in the early 1830s, with a population of more than 91,000, even though not as badly off as other rapidly growing industrial towns, such as Liverpool and Manchester where large numbers of the poorest residents lived in cellars, had its very densely populated areas, with most working-class residents living in back-to-back houses built in small groups around yards or 'courts'. These cottages, of which there were some 16,000 in the town by the early 1830s (and 38,000 by 1864 when further building of back-to-backs was outlawed by the new building bye-laws), comprised a cellar, a kitchen-living room with a paved floor on the ground floor, a bedchamber on the first floor where husband and wife and the younger children slept, and an attic under the eaves where the older children or a lodger slept. Each back-to-back cottage had neighbouring buildings sharing walls on three sides, usually other back-to-backs, but in some cases a wall may have been shared with a workshop, factory or public house. The arrangement meant that there were windows in only one of the four walls of the cottage facing either the street or the court, so there was no through ventilation. The poorest of the population did not even

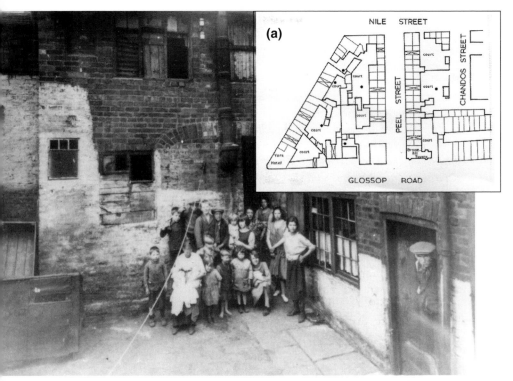

(b)

Early nineteenth century housing conditions in Sheffield (a) back-to-back housing in Peel Street with shared privies and water pumps. Ordnance Survey *(b) a crowded Sheffield court nearly a century after the outbreak of cholera in 1832. No wonder that contagious diseases spread quickly in such squalid and over-crowded housing conditions.* Sheffield City Libraries, Local Studies Library

attain this level of comfort; they were accommodated in the meanest hovels in the oldest parts of the town in abject squalor. On 3 December 1831, for example, the *Sheffield Independent* reported that one of the town's watchmen had entered a house called 'Mop Sam's' in 'the Isle' and in a room four yards by four yards and a half had found fifteen men and women huddled together; in the room above the watchmen counted fourteen more.

Cramped and often smelly as living conditions must have been in these hovels and the back-to-back cottages, it was not the internal arrangements that proved to be injurious or even fatal in terms of the cholera epidemic. It was the fact that each courtyard contained the communal privies and the standpipe or water pump for between two and a dozen cottages. There was a constant possibility of leakage from the privies and from the primitive drains into the drinking supply, especially in the flat and wet Ponds area, the low-lying and often flooded streets along the River Don above Lady's Bridge, and the densely packed streets and courts off Fargate, Snig Hill and Park Hill.

It is useful at this stage in the story to consider in more detail the supply of drinking water for Sheffield in the early 1830s. The original supplies must have come from the rivers and tributary streams, from springs and from wells. By the nineteenth century the rivers and most of the streams were polluted. In 1861, for example, thirty years after the cholera outbreak, *The Builder* magazine described Sheffield's rivers as being 'the conduits of all imaginable filth' and at one place 'positively run blood'. The article went on to say that the rivers were 'polluted with dirt, dust, dung and carrion; the embankments are ragged and ruined; here and there overhung with privies; and often the site of ash and offal heaps.' The writer concluded that the town was 'as devoid of the decencies of civilization as it was in the Dark Ages.'[7]

And yet from the second half of the eighteenth century great strides had been taken in Sheffield to supplement and eventually to supplant the drinking water supplies obtained from polluted rivers, and streams, and from small springs and public and private wells, by the construction of reservoirs to the west of the town and from which water was piped directly into people's homes. The earliest water collecting system, lay in the Crookesmoor valley and in 1832, the year of the cholera outbreak in Sheffield, J Tayler's map of the town shows the Great Dam and nine smaller reservoirs in the valley. From these dams the water was piped to a reservoir between Glossop Road and Brook Hill before being piped to houses in the town. But as late as 1843 there were still some 6,000 homes (out of 25,000) without piped water.

The Crookes reservoirs in 1832 from J Tayler's map of the town and its environs.

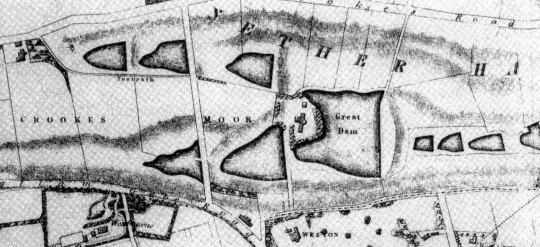

October 1831 – July 1832: the malignant disease at bay
A central Board of Health was set up by the government in June 1831, four months before the epidemic struck Britain. After the identification of the first cases in Sunderland on 19 October 1831, the Privy Council in London on 21 October suggested that each town should establish a Local Board of Health which should supervise the isolation of all cholera victims and burn their 'contaminated' clothing and other belongings. On 7 November Sheffield's Town Trustees set up a meeting for the 9 November of the Church Burgesses, the Churchwardens and Overseers of the Poor of the six townships within the parish of Sheffield, the Cutlers' Company, the Infirmary Board, the Magistrates, the Police and the town's leading medical practitioners to consider the means of 'preventing the Cholera or mitigating it should that malignant disease unfortunately appear in Sheffield'. A Provisional Committee was formed and the medical men were asked to form a Medical Board. The workhouse at Kelham Island was proposed as an isolation hospital because of its 'airiness and cleanliness and also from its being walled round'.[8] The Provisional Committee, which became the local Board of Health in 1832, met daily at the Cutlers' Hall and issued a broad range of advice. For example, in November 1831 they issued advice about ventilating homes ('from the garret to the cellar'); keeping bodies and properties clean of all 'emanations or effluvia'; cutting out bad habits – drinking ('Sobriety is here of the first moment') and smoking of tobacco ('a drug of the most pernicious nature') being especially highlighted; taking outdoor exercise ('one of the first practical duties of life'); getting enough sleep; and wearing the right clothing (let the wearers of light shoes and stockings beware; Cholera is no respecter of persons').[9] The chairman of Sheffield Board of Health was, for much of its existence, James Montgomery, the newspaper proprietor, poet and hymn writer.

On 12 November 1831 the *Sheffield Independent* announced that the local Board of Health had arranged for cartloads of lime to be sent to the poorest housing areas so that householders could whitewash their houses 'as a preservation against this dreadful malady'. The writer, however, thought it would be a 'dangerous experiment' to saturate the walls of rooms with lime and water where people would be sleeping within a few hours at 'this season of the year' – i.e., late Autumn, when windows would be closed. The newspaper also went on to caution against 'cholera phobia' that was likely to occur if fatal attacks of diarrhoea occurred amongst the 'poorer and worse fed' of the population.

As the months went by and the Spring and Summer of 1832 followed Winter, and although the disease occurred in Hull, Goole,

Kelham Island workhouse showing the upper floors that were used as a cholera isolation hospital.

York and Doncaster, it did not appear in the town and anxiety gradually subsided. Then on 16 June 1832 the *Sheffield Mercury* announced that:

> *We have reason to believe that a case of Spasmodic Cholera has occurred in the town. A person named Foster, who arrived a few days since from Thorne, was seized by some of the symptoms that distinguish this disease and died on Thursday – June 14.*

The newspaper went on to give this dire warning:

> *The Cholera is likely to come to Sheffield. It attacks chiefly the dirty, idle, the drunken, and the disorderly. Those, therefore, who wish to escape the Cholera should be sober, industrious, and steady and keep themselves and their houses clean.*

The medical authorities could not agree whether the death on 14 June was a case of cholera, expressing, as the *Sheffield Independent* reported, also on 16 June, 'various and contradictory opinions'. And the *Courant* newspaper went so far on 1 July 1832 as to proclaim in a leading article that 'The alarm is entirely groundless'. But this false note of optimism was short-lived.

In July, probably just before the epidemic reached Sheffield, the local poet, Paul Rodgers, wrote a poem entitled 'On the Approach of the Cholera Morbus'. The opening verse goes:

Oh, Britain! pride and wonder of the earth;
On thy tall cliffs a sound is heard from far;
Cease from thy revels and untimely mirth,
God comes in His own dreadful Judgement Car!

And continues:

Hark! From the North, the pestilential blast
Sweeps o'er the nations, prostrate with fear;
At its approach pale nature shrieks aghast,
And death and silence close its dread career.

July 1832 – November 1832: Cholera in Sheffield

The first confirmed case of cholera appeared in the town on 8 July. In a news report published on 14 July, the *Sheffield Independent*, after reporting two deaths in Derby and three in Nottingham, went on to state that:

In our own town (Sheffield) much alarm has been created during the week. We have received no official accounts from the Board of Health established here (and we have been solicited not to give publicity to any accounts of the progress of the disease without a certificate from the medical practitioners), but it appears that during the week three or four deaths have occurred under the circumstances that distinguish the spasmodic or Asiatic cholera.

Readers were assured that those suffering from the disease were being cared for in the hospital attached to the poorhouse. In the next week's issue (21 July) it was reported that twenty-five cases had occurred since 8 July, ten of these resulting in death. Striking an optimistic note, the report went on to say that 'the public will be glad to learn that the disease termed cholera has made little progress in the town.' It continued by stating that the 'temperate and orderly portion of society' had little to fear and that the 'poorer members of the community, who may probably be most liable to attack' would be taken care of most humanely and efficiently in the 'House of Recovery'.

Woodcock in his journal described the onset of the epidemic in Sheffield in July as follows:

A young Woman was attacked of the name of Mary Hodgson who lived in the neighbourhood of Ellin's Wheel, about the Bottom of Arundel

Street, she was taken in a Basket prepared for the Purpose, to the Cholera Hospital at the Workhouse, the day following, her Mother who lived in the same House was seized with the Disease & was conveyed to the Hospital where she died next Morning, the Daughter recovered though very slowly ...[10]

He went on to describe a whole family, the Bells (father, mother, two sons and one daughter), who lived on Walker Street in the Wicker, that was struck down by the disease:

The eldest Son was in a public House in Company with one of our Men (Samuel Howard) as late as ten o'clock at night, at one o'clock next Morning he was seized with Cholera and during the forenoon was removed to the Cholera Hospital about Noon the same day the youngest Son, a fine healthy lad, was taken ill & died in the evening, before Midnight the Father was attacked & died on the following Morning early, the Daughter was next day taken ill and was carried to the Hospital, the Mother was then advised by the Medical Attendant to quit the House they inhabited in order to avoid the Disease but she fell sick of it in a day or two after and died very shortly after being seized, the eldest Son and the Daughter who had been removed to the Hospital slowly recovered.[11]

Towards the end of July, there were signs that the disease was rapidly spreading to many different parts of the town. On 27 July, by which time there had been fifty cases and twenty-four deaths, the *Courant* recorded that cases had occurred as far apart as in the Park, on the Moor, at the bottom of Arundel Street, in Nursery Street, in Pond Street and nearby Pond Hill, Spring Street, Water Lane, the bottom of Furnival Street, and at Cotton Mill Row. On 17 August, by which time 630 cases had been reported and 207 deaths had occurred, the same newspaper reported that the worst affected areas were Park Hill, Bridgehouses and the Wicker. On

Walker Street at the far end of the Wicker where the Bell family lived as portrayed on J Tayler's map of the town and its environs in 1832.

22 August, in the middle of the month when the disease was most virulent, a Fast Day was celebrated 'to supplicate the Divine Throne for the remission of the Cholera'. For this occasion James Montgomery wrote a hymn, 'For a day of humiliation during the prevalence of the Cholera', the second and third verses summing up neatly the prevailing terror and helplessness:

> *Let priests and people, high and low,*
> *Rich, poor and great and small,*
> *Invoke in fellowship and woe,*
> *The Maker of them all.*

> *For God hath summoned from his place*
> *Death in a direr form,*
> *To waken, warn and scourge our race*
> *Than earthquake, fire or storm.*

By the end of August 1,086 cases had been reported and 342 deaths had occurred. During September there were just over 200 new cases and 48 deaths. But by the beginning of October the worst was over. On 5 October it was reported that the local Board of Health had suspended its daily sittings and members were meeting at intervals of a few days. A small number of cases continued to be reported during October and November and into early December, only one case being reported after 8 December. Things were so improved in November that on 22 November a Day of Thanksgiving was held with special church and chapel services throughout the town and James Montgomery wrote another special hymn , one of the lines being 'Now be sorrow turned to song'. Most of the dead were from the poorer end of society, but the District Committee's advice that cholera was no respecter of persons proved right in that the disease claimed one of the town's leading citizens, John Blake, Master Cutler who died on 30 August.

After 8 August burials in public graveyards was forbidden and from then on they took place in a special burial ground opposite the Shrewsbury almshouses in Norfolk Road where in 1834 the Cholera Monument was erected. From then on until the end of the epidemic a team of clergymen officiated at the funerals on a rota from nine in the morning until six in the evening for six days a week. The sound of the horses pulling the hearse, which became known as the 'cholera basket' would have been heard almost constantly.

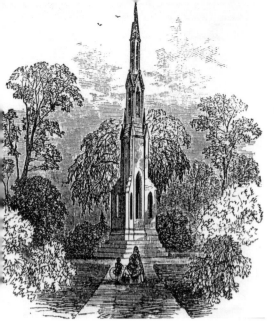

The Cholera monument. Illustrated Guide to Sheffield, Pawson & Brailsford, 1862

Life – life, is grown both dark and
    drear,
The earth is fill'd with gloom,
At every step we meet a bier
Slow wheeling to the tomb, -
That nameless tomb where hundreds
    lie
In one commingled heap –
Where few of all the passers-by
Dare pause awhile to weep.

So wrote another local poet, Mary Hutton.

Postscript

It was pointed out at the beginning of this chapter that the way cholera epidemics spread was not understood in the early 1830s. The problem was not solved until more than twenty years later when an epidemic in the Soho area of London was investigated by Dr John Snow. He published his findings in the second edition of his essay called 'On the Mode of Communication of Cholera'. In his essay he produced a map of what he called the 'cholera field' extending about 200 yards around a water pump in Broad Street. On this map he plotted the place of residence of the 500 people who died from cholera between 1 and 10 September 1854. Snow pointed out that most of the dead had been users of the Broad Street pump, whereas other people living in the same area but obtaining their water supply from elsewhere were unaffected. This was the first time a relationship between cholera and contaminated water had been proven.

The 'cholera field' around Broad Street pump, Soho, London, 1854.

'RIGHT SHEFFIELD IS BEST':
THE HISTORY OF SHEFFIELD'S
LIGHT STEEL TRADES

No account of the making of Sheffield would be complete without a long look at its two staple industries, the light steel trades and heavy steel manufacture and engineering which have sustained it for centuries. It is a story of making use of the region's natural resources, of tradition and holding on to age-old crafts and practices, of technical and organisational advance and backwardness, of taking advantage of new opportunities and overcoming locational disadvantage, of the triumph of home grown and imported inventive expertise and business acumen, and of brilliant progress, world leadership, followed by failure to adapt and finally of sharp contractions in the size of the two industries. This chapter looks at the evolution of the light steel trades and the next chapter discusses the heavy steel manufacturing industry and engineering.

Beginnings

No one knows when the light steel trades of Sheffield were born. The oft quoted thirteenth line of Geoffrey Chaucer's 'The Reeve's Tale' in his *The Canterbury Tales* – 'A scheffeld thwitel baar he in his hose' suggests that in the late fourteenth century (*The Canterbury Tales* were written between 1387 and 1400) the author believed that reference to 'a pointed Sheffield knife', used for cutting and spearing food and kept in a sheaf at the waist, would be as familiar to his readers then as a Bakewell Tart or Worcester Sauce would be today. If this is the case then it can be confidently said that in the late fourteenth century Sheffield already had a national reputation for its cutlery manufacture. That is, of course, provided Chaucer was speaking about Sheffield, Yorkshire! In 1946 Professor Hugh O'Neill, in his inaugural lecture when he took up the position of Professor of Metallurgy at Swansea University College, caused consternation in local circles by suggesting that Chaucer meant Sheffield, Sussex not Sheffield, Yorkshire. Professor O'Neill's case was roundly attacked and put down by Dr J E Oxley in a combative article published in 1951.[1] In his rebuttal of O'Neill's case, Oxley pointed out that it had been suggested that Chaucer found out about the Sussex Sheffield through riding on the Pilgrim's Way on the way to Canterbury. Oxley forcefully rebutted this, emphasising that this is not the route taken by the pilgrims in *The Canterbury Tales* and that the Pilgrim's Way is in fact a 'romantic antiquarianism' and was never used by pilgrims. More seriously still, he pointed out that O'Neill had only been able to provide evidence of iron making in the Sheffield, Sussex vicinity and had provided no evidence of cutlery manufacture, nor, in the period in question, had he been able to name a single person with the occupation or surname of 'cutler'. By contrast in the Yorkshire Sheffield, there is a reference as early as 1297 in the tax returns *of Robertus le coteler* - Robert the cutler.[2] By the late fourteenth century, about the time that *The Canterbury Tales* were being written, there were a good number of references to cutlery making and allied trades. In the Poll Tax Returns of 1378–79 for Sheffield and Handsworth, for example, twenty smiths were listed together with three taxpayers, Thomas Byrlay, Jonannes atte Well, and Thomas Hank, who were specifically described as cutlers. In neighbouring Ecclesfield six smiths were listed, together with Ricardus Hyngham, 'cutteler' and Johannes Scot, 'arismyth' (arrowsmith).[3]

Whatever the truth of Chaucer's reference to Sheffield in the late fourteenth century, by Elizabethan times the town had overtaken its provincial rivals at Thaxted in Essex and Salisbury in Wiltshire and lay second only to London in cutlery manufacture. The term cutlery embraced not only the making of knives but also other articles with a cutting edge such as scissors, shears, sickles and arrows (but not forks which until the second half of the seventeenth century were regarded as an Italian, and somewhat feminine, affectation). There is a number of convincing literary references to the importance and reputation of Sheffield's cutlery manufacturers. For example, John Leland, the topographical writer, who visited Sheffield in 1540, wrote that 'Ther be many smithes and cutelars in Hallamshire'.[4] And in 1569, the 6th Earl of Shrewsbury wrote to Lord Burghley, Queen Elizabeth's Secretary of State, informing him that he would be receiving 'a case of Hallamshire whittells, being such fruictes as my pore cuntrey affordeth with fame throughout this realm'.[5] In a similar vein Peter Bales in his *Writing Schoolemaster*, published in 1590, put his praise of Sheffield in verse in his chapter on choosing a penknife:

Provide a good knife; right Sheffield is best.
A razor is next, excelling the rest.

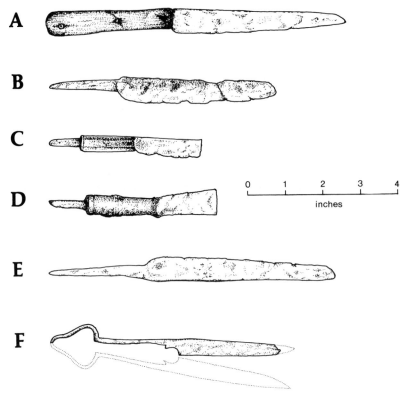

Knives and a pair of scissors found in the moat of Sheffield Castle during excavations between 1927–1929. A - sixteenth century knife; B - fifteenth century 'whittle' blade; C - late sixteenth or seventeenth century blade and bolster with traces of gilding on all the flat surfaces; D - late sixteenth or seventeenth cenury blade and bolster; E - fourteenth century 'whittle' blade; F - sixteenth century handle and blade of shear-shaped scissors. Re-drawn from A L Armstrong's drawings in his article 'Sheffield Castle: An account of Discoveries made during excavations on the site from 1927–29', Transactions of the Hunter Archaeological Society, IV, 1937

The author of the *Cobbler of Canterbury*, also published in 1590, wrote that:

> *Women's wittes are like Sheffield knives, for they are sometimes so keene as they will cutte a haire, and sometimes so blunte that they must goe to the grindstone.*[6]

As the cutlery trades of Sheffield and its surrounding area developed rapidly in the sixteenth century they came under the regulation of the manorial courts, which dealt with matters such as apprenticeships, the issuing of trade marks, the drawing up and supervision of work practice regulations and the settlement of disputes. Among the Cutlers' Ordinances (which were said to conform with the 'aunncyants' [ancient] ordinances and customs) drawn up in 1565, for example, were that no master could have more than one apprentice, that apprenticeships should be for seven years, and the banning of the making-up of parts supplied by craftsmen from outside the manor and the selling to outsiders of partly-finished articles.[7] There was, therefore, an organisational – and in many respects restrictive - framework within which the growing industry operated, together with the personal interest and patronage from successive lords of the manor, particularly from the 6th Earl of Shrewsbury (lord of the manor between 1560 and 1590) and the 7th Earl (1590–1616) under whose lordship new and more detailed ordinances were drawn up in 1590. The first marks known to have been recorded were in 1554 and by 1568 about sixty marks had been registered.

This organisational framework nurtured an industry which was based firmly on the exploitation of the local resources of coal measure ironstone from which the earliest metal articles were made, easily reached shallow coal seams and charcoal (from the large number of managed woods throughout the manor) for smelting and smithing fuel, grindstones from the coal measure sandstone quarries for putting the cutting edge on the finished articles, and, most importantly, the many water-powered sites that could be created on the fast flowing Don and its tributaries to power the forge hammers and grinding wheels. These local resources were supplemented by better-quality imported steel in the sixteenth century from northern Spain and in the seventeenth century from central Europe via the Rhine and the Baltic coasts of northern Germany, and from Sweden.

Knives recovered from the banks of the River Thames with what are probably Sheffield makers' marks. Top: Belly-bladed knife with carved bone handle bearing the mark probably granted to James Creswick by the Company of Cutlers in 1624; middle: small belly-bladed knife with a bone handle ending in a curved pistol grip bearing the mark probably granted to Joseph Parkin by the Manor Court in 1614; bottom: slope pointed knife with rootwood handle probably bearing the mark of Thomas Riche granted by the Manor Court in 1564. Courtesy of The Company of Cutlers of Hallamshire

Organisational change followed the death of the 7th Earl of
Shrewsbury in 1616. The Sheffield estate descended to Thomas
Howard, Earl of Arundel & Surrey who had married the 7th Earl's
youngest daughter Alethea. They did not live in Sheffield and the
Sheffield cutlers lost the personal interest of the new lord of the manor.
Two years before his death the 7th Earl had anticipated that changes
needed to be made in the affairs of Hallamshire's cutlers and he had
given permission for the jury of sixteen cutlers (which had been part of
the new ordinances of 1590) to issue marks. This semi-freedom and
autonomy made them take another step. They presented a successful
bill to Parliament in 1624. The bill – An Act for the Good Order and
Government of the Makers of Knives, Sickles, Shears, Scissors and
other Cutlery Wares, in Hallamshire, in the County of York, and the
parts near adjoining – was passed by the House of Commons in April
(with minor amendments) and by the House of Lords in May (without
amendment). Thus the Company of Cutlers in Hallamshire came into
being. At the time of the passing of the Act there were 498 master
craftsmen (440 knife makers, 31 shear and sickle makers and 27
scissors makers). Later in the century other specialist craftsmen were

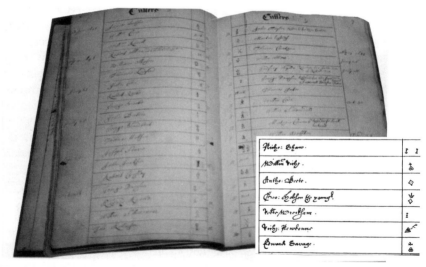

*The Great Mark Book of the Company of Cutlers which runs from 1678 to 1791
and contains more than 9,200 marks of cutlers, scissors-smiths, file-makers, shears
-smiths, scythe-makers and awl blade-makers.* Courtesy of the Company of Cutlers of
Hallamshire. ***Inset:*** *some of the cutlers' marks in the mark book of 1614, ten years
before the establishment of the Company of Cutlers.* R E Leader, The History of the
Company of Cutlers of Hallamshire, Volume 1, p 106

admitted and in 1682 when there were over 2,000 master craftsmen who had become members of the 'communality', they included scythe makers, file smiths and awl-blade makers.

By the mid-seventeenth century some sixty per cent of working men in Sheffield worked in the cutlery trades. Many of these workmen were 'little mesters' who ran their own businesses with the help of apprentices and journeymen (workers who had completed their apprenticeships but had not set up their own firms) from small workshops attached to their cottages. Here might be a coal-fuelled smithy where blades were forged or small rooms where the handles were fitted or 'hafted' and where knives were finally assembled after the blades had been taken to a riverside cutlers' wheel to be ground on a grindstone. Some cutlers might specialise in forging, grinding or assembling. The lists of personal possessions left in wills of the cutlers and those in related trades from Hallamshire and the surrounding district from the sixteenth and seventeenth centuries show clearly the nature and scale of the work undertaken. For example, in the will of 1510 of Thomas Parker, scythemaker, who had moved from Norton which was the main centre of scythe making in the district, to the Whitley valley in Ecclesfield parish, he left to his younger son the 'takke' [tenancy] of his 'watterwheles', a 'fourness' [furnace], 'ij stythies' [two anvils], his 'smithy gear', 'ij stoones'[two grindstones] and 'troughs called coltroughes' [stone troughs which were filled with water and in which a smith plunged red hot blades to cool them during the hardening process]. To his elder son, besides bequeathing him the copyhold of his land, Thomas left at the wheel in the Whitley valley two coltroughs, an anvil and a pair of bellows.[8] Nearly two centuries later the story was much the same: in 1694 cutler Charles

The interior of a grinding hull. The process of grinding did not change for centuries and working conditions were most unhealthy. The main cause of death among grinders was 'grinders' asthma' caused by inhaling stone and metal dust. In the 1830s life expectancy among fork grinders, who ground 'dry', was only 28–32 years. The Graphic, 28 November, 1874

Stewardson died and the inventory of the tools in his two-storeyed workshop listed seven vices, a glaser (a leather-covered wooden wheel dressed with emery cake for finishing blades), six pairs of boring stoops, wire and a parcel of tortoiseshell for knife hafts; and in 1718 John Winter's smithy tools included an anvil, a pair of bellows and thirty pound in shell for use in hafting.[9]

The existence of fast-flowing streams from the Pennines which could be exploited many times at short intervals during their course through the district gave Sheffield and surrounding parishes a critical advantage over their provincial rivals during the seventeenth century and over London and their foreign rivals by the end of the eighteenth century. By 1637, for example, when John Harrison undertook his survey of the manor of Sheffield he was able to report in his general description of the manor on the significance of the 'River of Doune', 'ye Sheaf' and the other Sheffield rivers which he called 'Porter Water, Loxley Water & Riveling Water with other small Rivers & Brookes'. These rivers, he said,

> ... *are very profitable unto ye Lord in regard of the Mills* [i.e., water-powered corn mills] *& Cutler wheeles that are turned by theire streames, which weeles are imployed for the grinding of knives by four or five hindred Master Workmen that gives severall marks.*

In the survey itself he listed rents from thirty-one 'Cutler Wheeles'.[10] It has been estimated that there were about fifty water-powered industrial sites on Sheffield's rivers by 1660, that this had risen to about ninety by 1740 and to about 130 by the end of the eighteenth century, after which only a handful of new sites were created. At the height of the use of water-power on Sheffield's rivers they occurred on average four times on every mile of river.

The usual method of harnessing water-power on Sheffield's rivers was that a weir was built to deflect water from the river into a reservoir, locally called a dam, via a channel called a head goit or leat. The dam was generally parallel to the river but at a higher level. Water was led from the dam onto a vertical water-wheel, and then flowed away, via a tail goit, to rejoin the river downstream. When the fall of water was over about ten feet an overshot wheel was normal, with the water hitting the wheel close to the top. Where the fall of water was lower, a breast wheel would be used with the water feeding it lower down. Very low falls of water fed undershot wheels with the stream often flowing directly under the wheel. Undershot wheels were rare in the Sheffield area but one survives at Malin Bridge Mill.

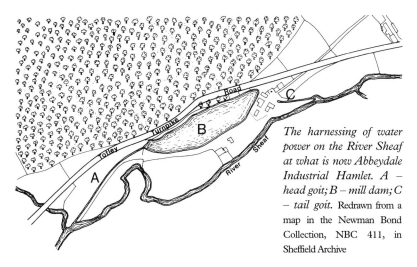

The harnessing of water power on the River Sheaf at what is now Abbeydale Industrial Hamlet. A – head goit; B – mill dam; C – tail goit. Redrawn from a map in the Newman Bond Collection, NBC 411, in Sheffield Archive

By the end of the seventeenth century Sheffield knives and edge tools were not only sold throughout Britain and Ireland but had penetrated markets abroad, reaching the mainland of Europe, the West Indies and the North American colonies. And in Europe they were sold well off the beaten track. John Spencer (1655–1729) of Cannon Hall, for example, besides being a major landowner, farmer and industrialist also had merchant interests in the Baltic region. In the late 1680s and early 1690s he is known to have been exporting 'Sheffield wares' including knives, penknives, spring knives and forks, some with tortoiseshell and others with horn handles, razors with silver capped handles, inkpots and buttons, from Hull to Narva, a port on the southern shores of the Gulf of Finland in the most eastern part of the Baltic Sea in modern-day Estonia, almost 1,200 miles from Sheffield. From there they were probably distributed in Finland and possibly Russia. His agent in the Baltic also brought goods to Stockholm in Sweden and even mentioned travelling north into Lapland.[11]

Crucible steel, silver plate and steam power
Until the second half of the eighteenth century the steel used by Sheffield's cutlers was either imported, as noted above, or was locally made 'shear steel' which was forged from 'blister steel' made in a cementation furnace. Thomas Oughtibridge's view of Sheffield in 1737 shows two cementation furnaces, easily recognised by their conical chimneys. Some 260 such furnaces were eventually built in the Sheffield area, of which only one survives. In a cementation

furnace in two sandstone chests were put alternate layers of charcoal and iron bars covered by a layer of mortar made from 'wheelswarf', the debris of sand and steel grindings from the bottom of a grinder's trough. The furnace was sealed and a coal fire lit below the sandstone chests which burned for seven to nine days. After about a week of cooling down the furnace was opened and the iron bars now converted to blister steel (they were covered in small blisters) were removed. Incidentally, the hard crust from the top of the chests called 'crozzle' can still be seen topping walls throughout the Sheffield area. The bars of blister steel were then converted into shear steel by being heated in bundles to bright red and then forged into a uniform bar. Sometimes while still hot a bar of shear steel was cut in two and re-forged to make 'double-shear steel'. Shear steel could be ground to produce a sharp cutting edge but was still not completely uniform in carbon content and therefore uniformity and was not suitable for all steel products.

This led to the development of crucible steel by Benjamin Huntsman in the 1740s. Born of Quaker parents in Epworth just across the boundary of south Yorkshire in Lincolnshire in 1705, Huntsman became a clockmaker in Doncaster in 1725. He was dissatisfied with the quality of steel available to him for making clock springs so he experimented in producing a homogeneous steel without variations in carbon content. He moved to Handsworth in order, it is believed, to obtain supplies of coking coal and refractory clays and possibly to gain knowledge of furnace practice from the glassmakers of Catcliffe, less than two miles away. His experiments in Handsworth involved devising a way of re-melting blister steel to create an almost 'pure' steel of consistent quality for clock spring making. To do this he put broken bars of blister

The sole surviving cementation furnace in Sheffield. Joan Jones. **Inset:** *detail from Thomas Oughtibridge's View of Sheffield, 1737, showing two early cementation furnaces.*

Huntsman's Steel Works in Attercliffe in the late nineteenth century, with three cone-shaped cementation furnaces on the left and the broad, rectangular-shaped chimneys of the crucible furnaces on the right. Sheffield and Neighbourhood, Pawson & Brailsford, 1889

steel in small clay pots (crucibles) in a coke fire at very high temperatures (1,550–1,650 degrees fahrenheit) for up to five hours. What he in fact produced was the ideal steel for cutlery and edge tool making. By 1751 he had moved to Attercliffe to take up the full time occupation of steelmaker. Although the introduction of crucible steel was at first resisted by Sheffield's cutlers who said it was hard to work, eventually it resulted not only in the world-wide renown of the Sheffield cutlery industry but also in the growing international reputation of Sheffield as a steel making centre. By about 1850 ninety per cent of the country's steel (crucible steel) was made in Sheffield and nearly fifty per cent of all the steel made in Europe was Sheffield made.

The process of making crucible or cast steel, as it was sometimes known, particularly the final part of the process which was pure theatre, has taken on an almost mythical quality, celebrated in drawing, engraving, painting and

Crucible teemer. From an advertisement for Sheffield Climax Steel Co Ltd, Arundel Street, Sheffield, 1919

Thomas Boulsover. A Gatty, Sheffield Past and Present, 1873, p 137

sculpture (at Meadowhall shopping centre). After some three hours in the underground furnace the 'puller-out', wearing protective leggings, a sacking apron and a glove on the hand used to hold the tongs nearest the 'fire hole', moved to one side the top of the fire hole, inserted his long tongs and skilfully removed the glowing crucible from the mass of brightly burning coke, placed it on the floor, and removed the lid. The head melter or 'teemer', like the puller-out protected by leggings, apron and gloved hand, then lifted the crucible with tongs, using his thigh as a fulcrum, and poured the red hot metal into a waiting ingot mould which was thirty inches high and only three inches by three inches wide. The skill and strength involved in the intense heat (the combined weight of crucible, steel and tongs being about 100 pounds) was immense. One contemporary observer said the process was very beautiful when performed at night.

While Huntsman was making his experiments in steel making in Handsworth another development that would have an immense impact on Sheffield's light industries was taking place in Norfolk Street in Sheffield. Thomas Boulsover (1704–88), a cutler, was repairing a knife whose handle was made of silver and copper when he realised that a thin sheet of silver could be fused together with copper to give the impression of solid silver. Boulsover had to roll and craft his plated silver, which became known as Old Sheffield Plate, by hand but soon other firms were entering the trade and during the second half of the eighteenth century firms such as John Hoyland & Co, Joseph Hancock, and Tudor, Leader and Sherburn became major manufacturers of a wide range of plated silver articles including snuff boxes, pocket flasks, buckles, buttons, candlesticks, and a wide range of fancy 'holloware' such as coffee pots, jugs, dishes, bowls and trays.

White metal or Britannia metal as it became more widely known, composed of tin, brass, copper and a small amount of antimony was invented about 1769 by James Vickers and this new alloy took over

Silver and gilt tea and coffee service by James Dixon & Sons exhibited at the Great Exhibition at Crystal Palace in 1851. The design of the service is based on the pitcher plant and the tray on a leaf of the giant water lily, Victoria regia. Illustrated Catalogue of the Great Exhibition, 1851

the lower end of the market as a substitute for pewter. Because the manufacture of articles in silver plate, Britannia metal and then solid silver involved substantial capital investment, these branches of the light trades were among the first to fully embrace the idea of an integrated factory-based operation with specialist craftsmen recruited from all parts of the country. So important had the manufacture of articles in solid silver become by the 1770s that Sheffield was granted permission in 1773 to open an assay office.[12]

The last major innovation of the eighteenth century came in 1786 when steam power was applied to the grinding process. This had a number of important consequences. First it led to the gradual abandonment of many water-powered sites, one estimate suggesting that the number of water-powered sites shrank from more than 130 in 1770 to about thirty a hundred years later.[13] The new steam-powered workshops were overwhelmingly concentrated in the town of Sheffield itself mainly around the western edges of the built-up area and they later colonised the former Alsop Fields area on the valley slopes above the River Sheaf to the south of the existing town, an area laid out on a grid-iron plan by the principal landowner and lord of the manor, the Duke of Norfolk, between 1771 and 1778. The concentration of an increasing volume of the industry's capacity in an urban setting enabled the workmen to work at their trades full-time throughout the year, unworried by possible loss of power during the

dry, hot, summer months and uninterrupted by farming activities.
But craft techniques did not change in the traditional branches of the
industry with the result that the industry remained, to a large extent,
in small units.

The golden years of Sheffield's light steel trades

The nineteenth century saw much expansion in the number of
manufacturers and workers as markets grew and grew, and the
range of products multiplied. For the first three-quarters of the
century Sheffield was the steel and steel products capital of the
world. The period also saw the declining influence of the Cutlers'
Company, the invention of electro-plating to supersede Old
Sheffield plate, the introduction of artificial hafting materials such
as celluloid (introduced in 1868) ebonite, vulcanite and xylonite,
and the slow substitution of the integrated factory and mechanised
operations in place of the small smithy and workshop and
traditional hand crafts.

Market expansion not only took place domestically, but also
internationally, especially in the Empire and the United States, and to
a lesser extent in Europe and South America. Transport developments
were crucial. In the seventeenth and eighteenth centuries, the products
of the Sheffield light trades industry were moved to their markets by
packhorse with as many as fifty at a time leaving the town for the ports
of Yorkshire and Lancashire. Goods for the London and European
market went to the river port of Bawtry where they were transferred to
barges and carried down the River Idle to the Trent and the port of
Hull. The inconvenience and slowness of the overland journey from
Sheffield to Bawtry led the Cutlers' Company to explore the possibility
of making the Don navigable from Doncaster to Sheffield and in 1726
an Act of Parliament was passed and work began. But it proved
impracticable at the time to extend the waterway beyond Tinsley and
so Tinsley remained the terminus from 1751 until the late date of 1819
when the Sheffield canal opened, terminating at the Canal Basin near
the junction of the Sheaf and Don. The first railway to reach Sheffield
came only nineteen years later, but it was only a branch line, the
Sheffield and Rotherham Railway which connected the town at
Rotherham to the Midland Railway's main line from York to London
via Derby. This was followed by the trans-Pennine route of the
Manchester, Sheffield and Lincolnshire Railway which terminated in
Sheffield in 1845, the line being extended to Grimsby in 1847.
Sheffield then had to wait until 1870 before getting its direct railway
route to London which terminated at the then Midland Station. But

expanding production and the rapidly growing export trade had preceded the coming of the railways by several decades.

The biggest foreign market which had emerged in the eighteenth century even before the North American colonies gained their independence, was in the United States.[14] The population of the United States was only three million in 1786 but as migrants poured into the new country in the nineteenth century, and spread westwards, it had risen to thirty-one million by 1860, and with its own manufacturing industry still in its infancy, the demand for Sheffield steel and the products of its light steel trades must have seemed never ending. As Alfred Gatty, writing in his *Sheffield Past and Present*, published in 1873, put it:

> The settler needed his axe to fell the primeval forest, his spade to break the hitherto untilled ground, his saw, and chisel, and file, and scythe, and shears for constant use in building and in agriculture, as well as the necessary domestic utensils in setting up a new home. These and the like were the very things which Sheffield could at once supply, and it did so to a very large extent – insomuch that some few houses of business in Sheffield had established their agents at New York before the commencement of the present century, and the result was that its prosperity became most closely linked with the fortunes of America.[15]

Fortunes were made based on the American trade by firms such as W & S Butcher, James Dixon & Sons, William Greaves, Mappin Brothers, Marsh Brothers, Joseph Rodgers & Sons, and George Wostenholm & Son. Some firms even went as far as naming their new works after the American trade, for example George Wostenholm's Washington cutlery works, Brookes & Crookes' Atlantic cutlery works and Alfred Beckett's Brooklyn saw works.

But as markets rapidly expanded, technology and industrial organisation virtually stood still. As has already been pointed out, at the end of the eighteenth century, the concept of the factory was foreign to Sheffield's staple industries and the 'little mester's smithy' or workshop was the typical unit of manufacture in most branches. Here independent workmen worked, sometimes for several well-known names whose trademarks were stamped on the finished products. There were also 'public-wheels' or tenement factories whose owners supplied working space and power to 'out-workers' in return for a weekly rent. The out-workers were not tied to a particular master and they often worked for several at the same time, with the help of apprentices and skilled journeymen.

The ivory store at Joseph Rodgers & Sons. A great variety of raw materials was used for the hafts of knives and tools. The native woods ash and beech were widely used for tradesman's knives and tools. For cutlery the imported woods ebony and rosewood were widely employed, together with ivory, bone, horn, deer antler, porcelain, tortoiseshell, mother of pearl and abalone. By the end of the 1870s ivory cost about £1,000 per ton. The Graphic, 28 November, 1874

In the few factories that did exist in the first half of the nineteenth century it was not uncommon for a skilled artisan to take in work from outside, while it was usual for some men to pay a weekly rent and work completely independently. Many of the well-known firms depended more on the fame of their trade marks than on vast numbers of workmen in one all-purpose factory. The first integrated factory was the Sheaf Works near the canal basin built in 1823 for William Greaves, manufacturer of steel, razors and cutlery mainly for the American market, and later taken over by Thomas Turton & Sons who manufactured saws, files, edge tools and railway springs. This was followed by the Globe Works built for the Ibbotson Brothers between 1825–30. By 1850 integrated factories were also operated by two of Sheffield's most famous cutlery manufacturers, Joseph Rodgers & Son, at the Norfolk Works, and George Wostenholm & Son at the Washington Works; and by one of the two leading plate manufacturers, James Dixon & Sons, at Cornish Place. By the 1860s Wostenholm's Washington Works employed 800 people and in the 1880s James Dixon's plate works had 700 employees. As the century advanced, and some processes became mechanised more and more

George Wostenholm's Washington Works, erected in 1848. Sheffield and Neighbourhood, Pawson & Brailsford, 1889

factories, small, medium and large, were built. But machine-made articles were considered to be inferior by many manufacturers and craftsmen and mechanisation took place much more slowly in the Sheffield area than in the United States and Germany. In the United States, for example, with a shortage of labour, weak unions and no craft traditions, mechanised operations were used almost from the start and by the 1870s the American light steel trades, based largely in New England, had grown large enough to compete aggressively with imported Sheffield goods. The American trade was also hit by the imposition of tariffs on imported goods by successive US governments after the Civil War in 1865 and the particularly crippling McKinley tariff of 1890 almost killed the trade.

Trade depressions and trade outrages
The rapid expansion of the Sheffield light steel trades in the first half of the nineteenth century continued, with periodic minor depressions, until the mid-1870s. After that there were a series of depressions, some very severe, resulting from the loss of American markets, continental competition from France and Germany, and opposition among most of the trade unions in Sheffield to the introduction of labour-saving machinery and factory organisation which meant that changes in methods of production took longer than in rival foreign centres.

The most severe period of depression was in the period from 1874 to 1879. In 1879, for example, when trade was at its lowest ebb, firms were only working one or two days each week. The winter of 1878–79 was a very severe one. William Nesbitt, a Cumberland man who came to work for Newton Chambers at Thorncliffe in 1869 and who kept a diary of local events and was a meticulous recorder of local weather, said the severe winter had lasted from late November to the middle of April. On 15 March 1879 he noted that he believed that there had never been such a harsh winter in the 'present generation of man'. Ice on local dams and ponds was twelve inches thick in December and so many people went skating that the skate makers of Sheffield ran out of stock! The local economy, already in one of its deepest depressions of the century, was heavily disrupted and the unemployed and poor were in desperate need of support. He reported that £12,000 had been collected to relieve the stress of the poor in the town.[16]

Matters were widely reported in the local press and caught the attention of *The Illustrated London News,* the latter reporting that work had been found for the unemployed in the recreation grounds and on road building work, but comprehensive as that was, it could not employ half of those looking for work and 'hundreds of applicants had to be turned away'. It went on to say that some of the unemployed were in 'a pitiable condition' and 'starving for want of food'.

Sheffield's light trades, particularly the grinding trades, had also been brought to national attention in the 1850s and 1860s because of what became known as the 'Sheffield Outrages' and the widespread occurrence of 'rattening'. Rattening, a term thought to be derived from the meaning of rats entering buildings and taking away or destroying human belongings, took on the more notorious meaning in the nineteenth century in Sheffield's light trades of confiscating a workman's tools, most specifically the wheelband that

Feeding Sheffield's poor during the depression in the winter of 1878–79. The Illustrated London News, 18 January, 1879

attached his grindstone to the water wheel or steam engine and thus made it impossible for him to carry on his work and cut the supply of work to others engaged in related processes. Rattening was done by and on behalf of the 'trade societies' or unions in order to bring workmen into line by persuading them to join a union, pay fees that were owing to it or to make them stop working for a master who was paying less than the recommended rate. Rattening was usually followed by a threatening letter signed by 'Mary Ann'. What must be remembered was that until 1871, trade unions were virtually illegal, and so union leaders and officials had no legal right to ask members to pay regular subscriptions. They saw this as a one-sided approach by the government with the working classes treated as outlaws. So the unions resorted to blackmail. And no legal proceedings followed because there was a conspiracy of silence.

However, matters took a decided turn for the worse in the 1850s and 1860s. A saw grinder was shot at in 1854; a gunpowder attack took place on a file grinder in 1857; four fender grinders were physically assaulted and a saw grinder murdered by shooting in 1859; a knife grinder was physically assaulted in 1861 and in the same year a gunpowder attack on the home of a fender grinder led to the death of an innocent woman lodger in the house; and gunpowder attacks took place on a sickle grinder in 1865 and on a saw grinder in 1866.

It was not until after the 1866 outrage, which took place in October (and in which damage was relatively minor) that official action taken. £1,900 was raised to compensate the saw grinder and a reward of £1,000 was offered by employers for evidence leading to the capture of the perpetrator of the crime. But to no avail. Silence continued to prevail. Then a deputation went from Sheffield to the Home Office representing the Town Council, the Cutlers' Company, the Chamber of Commerce, and a manufacturers' protection society to demand a commission of inquiry into the affair. This was followed by a deputation from the Sheffield trade unions to make the same request.

A commission of inquiry was set up early in 1867 to cover Sheffield and Manchester where there had been similar outrages. The Sheffield commission, which began its work in June 1867, was given authority to investigate outrages during the preceding ten years and to give certificates of indemnity to witnesses in return for their evidence. The proceedings lasted for five weeks. On the twelfth day one of the men who had been paid to carry out a number of assaults (including the shooting of the saw grinder in 1859), James Hallam, an unemployed saw grinder, broke down and confessed. Later that day his partner in crime, Samuel Crookes, also confessed, and the next day so did the instigator of the assaults, William Broadhead, landlord of the *Royal George* in Carver Street and Treasurer of the Associated Trades of Sheffield.

The commission found evidence of 166 cases of rattening and twenty-one cases of sending threatening letters, and that twelve of the sixty trade unions in the town had been involved in these cases. Rattening did not stop immediately (fifty-six cases were reported in the local newspapers between 1867 and 1887) and a number of trade unions stood by their officials who had been implicated in outrages. The Trades Union Act of 1873 legalised the trade unions. In more recent times the whole matter was brilliantly dramatised as *The Stirrings in Sheffield on Saturday Night* by Allan Cullen, first produced at the Playhouse theatre in 1966.

The light trades at the end of the nineteenth century

William Broadhead. Sheffield City Libraries, Local Studies Library

In 1911 there were approximately 35,000 persons employed in the light steel trades in Sheffield, an increase of thirty-nine per cent on 1851, but of only eight per cent on 1891. This slow recent growth was not indicative of a decline in the industry, which had in fact continued to grow steadily, if unevenly, in spite of the virtual loss of the United States market – it was a reflection of the increasing mechanisation of the industry.

By the beginning of the twentieth century electric motors were becoming common in the industry, and the forging of file blades, the cutting of files, the filing of forks and the grinding of saws had all been mechanised. In the electro-plating industry the rolling and stamping of products were also done by machine. There were still, however, large numbers of hand workers in the light trades, particularly for the production of luxury articles.

Mechanisation had come slowly to Sheffield, taking almost half a century. Technical progress in the industry was hampered by tradition, and by the trade societies which strongly opposed the adoption of machines. Saw and file making typified the problem.

Saw-grinding machinery was introduced in the USA as early as 1858[17] but it was not until 1867 that grinding machines were installed for the first time in Sheffield, and it was not until the last decade of the nineteenth century that machines were employed to do the paring, grinding and teething of saws. In the file trade American firms had mechanised all their processes by 1865 and machines were used in England at Oldham and Manchester about the same time. In Sheffield a grinding machine was installed in 1865 and immediately aroused the opposition of the local trade societies. The workers refused to complete the work begun by the machine, and they objected to non-union men being employed to work the machine. There followed a sixteen-week file strike which failed, and machines were then introduced, but they did not become firmly established until the 1880s.

File-making factories in Sheffield continued to employ out-workers making hand-cut files, and who in a dwindling number of cases in the surrounding rural area continued in the ancient tradition of combining their trade with a rural occupation.[18] But inevitably employment in file-making in the Sheffield area declined from 6,200 in 1891 to 4,850 in 1911. Contraction in employment in the same

A hand-cut file maker's workshop. Note that the file being cut is laid on a block of lead and secured by leather straps held in position by a stirrup on the filemaker's left foot. The chisel is hit by a characteristically curved-handled mallet. The Illustrated London News, 10 March, 1866

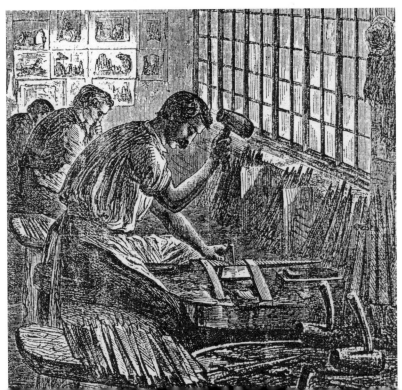

period was typical of most branches of the light trades, the exception being the silver and silver plate trades where there had been no change in the methods of production in the second half of the nineteenth century, employment climbing from 5,500 in 1851 to 10,600 in 1911.

The gradual disappearance of the 'little mester' from the industrial scene was to be expected as the mechanisation of the light steel trades became more widespread. Lack of capital made it difficult for them to install machinery, and they were far more vulnerable to the repeated depressions of the last quarter of the century. However, many small firms did survive, chiefly because they found it possible to adapt themselves quickly to changing designs and fashions and because they were able to make small batches of products of a particular design for a particular market, long after that design had been superseded in the larger mechanised firms.

As late as 1896 it was estimated that there were 170 tenement factories in the city with 2,900 tenants, and in 1908 Home Office returns were obtained from 378 factories, including 155 tenement factories with 2,597 tenants.[19] The extent to which the very small firm and the outwork system was still typical of the industry may be seen from the Factory Returns of 1904. These reveal that the 15,970 cutlery workers over eighteen years of age in the United Kingdom in that year, most of whom worked in Sheffield, worked in 2,752 establishments – an average of five males and one female per establishment![20] In contrast to this, at the other end of the scale in the 1890s Joseph Rodgers & Sons employed 2,000 workers and four other firms – George Wostenholm, James Dixon, Walker & Hall and Mappin & Webb – employed nearly 1,000 each.

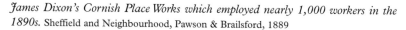

James Dixon's Cornish Place Works which employed nearly 1,000 workers in the 1890s. Sheffield and Neighbourhood, Pawson & Brailsford, 1889

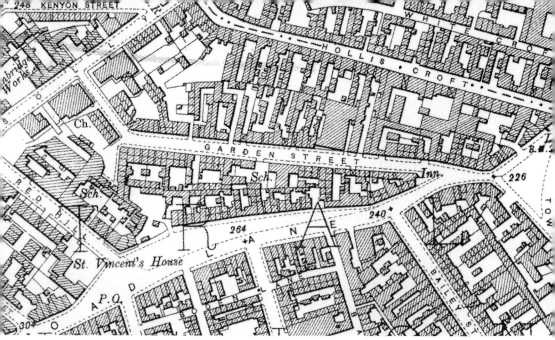

Part of the Sheffield light trades quarter in 1903. Hollis Croft at that time contained the small factories and workshops of a buff and glaser manufacturer, two haft and scale cutters, and makers of electro-plate, pocket knives, butchers' knives, table knives, forks, files and saws. Nearby Garden Street contained three electro-plate manufacturers, four cutlery makers, a German silver founder, two file makers, a scissors maker and a gimlet maker. Ordnance Survey 25 inches to one mile sheet, 1903

Although at the very end of the nineteenth century there were still substantial numbers of light steel trades workmen in small and medium-sized firms in the rural and semi-rural areas surrounding Sheffield – including, for example, 1,854 cutlery workers and 1,152 file workers in 1901 – the industry by this time was largely urbanised in Sheffield. It occupied an area, with large and medium-sized factories mixed with a complex of small workshops and back-to-back housing, almost completely surrounding the central retail, office and entertainment area. This area stretched in an anti-clockwise direction from the confluence of the Don and Sheaf westwards on the flat land to the south of the River Don to the Royal Infirmary and beyond and then swept southwards mainly to the east of St Philip's Road until it reached the Porter Brook at Little London; it then turned northwards down the valley of the Sheaf, including the valley slopes on the east and west above the valley floor back to the confluence of the Sheaf with the Don.

A century of boom, depression, and downward spiral
A major scientific breakthrough came in 1913 when Harry Brearley, director of Brown-Firth's research laboratories discovered a chromium

steel which almost completely resisted corrosion. In his biography *Knotted String*, published in 1941, Brearley, who came from a poor Sheffield background (he was born in Ramsden's Yard off the Wicker) and was largely self-taught, wrote that he had been taken on after leaving school as a bottle washer in Firth's laboratory by the chemist 'because my face was cleaner than another's'. His ground-breaking discovery changed the face of cutlery manufacture after the First World War. His 'rustless steel', as it was first called, when tried by local cutlers was disliked at first – just as they had disliked crucible steel when it first made its appearance 170 or so years earlier – because it was difficult to forge using traditional methods. Power-forging solved the problem and the first stainless steel knives were produced for sale in late 1914. But the discovery coincided with the outbreak of the First World War, and the government insisted that a more strategic use of stainless steel must prevail – the manufacture of aeroplane engine parts for the flying machines of the Royal Flying Corps.

Cutlery manufacturers, therefore, spent the war years in full production of army knives, bayonets, steel helmets, cutlery and razors for soldiers, sailors and airmen and other military equipment. Tool

Harry Brearley, discoverer of stainless steel in 1913, being presented the Freedom of the City of Sheffield in 1939. Sheffield City Libraries, Local Studies Department. **Inset:** *the blade of an early stainless steel carving knife by John Round & Son with the label 'Firth Brearley Stainless' etched into it.*

A sample of the vast array of steel tools made in Sheffield in the nineteenth century.
Advertisement in White's Sheffield District Directory, 1893

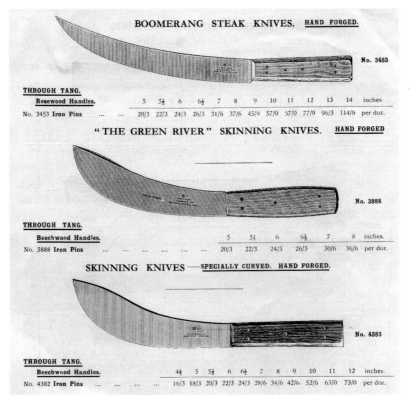

BOOMERANG STEAK KNIVES. HAND FORGED.

No. 3453

THROUGH TANG.

Rosewood Handles.	5	5½	6	6½	7	8	9	10	11	12	13	14	inches
No. 3453 Iron Pins	20/3	22/3	24/3	26/3	31/6	37/6	45/9	57/0	57/0	77/9	96/3	114/6	per doz.

"THE GREEN RIVER" SKINNING KNIVES. HAND FORGED

No. 3888

THROUGH TANG.

Beechwood Handles.	5	5½	6	6½	7	8	inches.
No. 3888 Iron Pins	20/3	22/3	24/3	26/3	30/6	36/6	per doz.

SKINNING KNIVES —SPECIALLY CURVED. HAND FORGED.

No. 4382

THROUGH TANG.

Beechwood Handles.	4½	5	5½	6	6½	7	8	9	10	11	12	inches.
No. 4382 Iron Pins	16/3	18/3	20/3	22/3	24/3	28/6	34/6	42/6	52/6	63/0	73/0	per doz.

Despite a long depression Sheffield was still producing traditional goods by the old methods at the end of the 1930s. This page from an illustrated price list of 1940 shows a small part of the range of butchers' and provision dealers' cutlery knives produced under the name of John Wilson, of Sycamore Street, a firm which had been founded in 1750. The first page of the price list proclaimed that all the products were made from ' the Finest Guaranteed Double Shear Steel – Hand Forged'.

manufacturers also diverted their production to military markets. Silver and electro-silver manufacturing disappeared for the duration, many former employees either joining up in the armed forces or obtaining jobs in the heavy steel industry. The war was followed by a short-lived boom followed by a severe slump which began in 1921 and lasted until rearmament began in the second half of the 1930s. In this period stainless steel became the premier steel for cutlery making and steel made in electric-arc and induction furnaces became the main raw material among the leading tool makers. An interesting feature of the 1930s is that the period saw the rise to prominence of three cutlery firms headed by immigrants from Germany. The oldest of these, was Viners (an Anglicised version of the German-Jewish name Viener) who had settled in Sheffield about 1900 and established a silver and silver plate company. The firm specialised in plated holloware and flatware and gradually took over a number of small firms that were in difficulties and employed their former owners as managers. By the end of the 1930s they had a workforce of about 1,000. The Sippel brothers came to England in 1931 to help in the mechanisation of the cutlery industry,and after operating from London initially they settled in Sheffield in 1933. They set up a factory in Arundel Street and later moved to Cadman Street where they specialised in the production of forks and spoons. By the outbreak of the Second World War they had a workforce of 400. A second two-brother partnership was formed by the Richartz brothers (Stephan who came to set up the company in 1932 and Paul who joined Stephan in 1937), from a cutlery manufacturing family in Solingen, who set up a pocket-knife company. The name was anglicised to Richards. By the outbreak of war they also employed about 400 workers. All three firms were to do well in the immediate post-war period.

The six years of the Second World War saw a reversion to the role played by the light trades in the First World War – with cutlery firms fulfilling government contracts for steel helmets, army knives, cutlery for the NAAFI and literally thousands of other types of war equipment including aeroplane parts, gun components, smoke bombs, parachute flares and mine prodders. The tool firms, besides increasing production of such items as spades and shovels, trenching tools, spanners and files, made enormous quantities of forgings and stampings for aircraft, tanks and many other war vehicle components including aircraft undercarriage parts.

Following the end of the war there was another boom which lasted until the second half of the 1950s. But by this time foreign competition in the cutlery industry was biting hard, not only from the traditional foreign rivals of the United States, France and Germany but also from the Far East from Japan which was followed in the 1960s by firms in Hong Kong and Taiwan and in the 1970s in South Korea, all producing their products at far below the prices of Sheffield cutlery. Various commentators during this period pointed out the weaknesses of the cutlery industry in Sheffield: it possessed few advantages of scale (in 1957 there were 650 cutlery firms in the UK, 450 of them in Sheffield) and management was said to be weak, complacent and inward looking. The knowledge and use of marketing techniques were said to be non-existent. To cut costs, some firms began to import blanks from the Far East and stamped Sheffield marks on the finished products.

The crash came in the early 1970s, and it was not only the small very vulnerable firms that went out of business, but also the bigger

Viner's cutlery factory being demolished. Peter Machan

Peter Goss, little mester, who has worked at Kelham Island Industrial Museum since 1988. Peter is a surgical instrument maker specialising in the production of hand-forged forceps, chisels, hip replacements and bone levers. Joan Jones

firms that had survived through thick and thin for many years.
Wostenholm's were taken over by Joseph Rodgers in 1971, this
combine was itself bought by Richards Brothers in the mid-1970s,
but by the early 1980s Richards' themselves were declared
bankrupt. Sippel's, one of the three growing German firms in the
inter-war period went out of business in 1972 and Viner's, the
largest cutlery firm in the country went out of business in 1982, its
name and trade mark were sold and, shamefully, it now appears on
imported Korean cutlery. The silver and electro-plate companies
fared no better: the well-known firms of Walker & Hall, James
Dixon, Atkin Brothers and Cobb and Cooper Brothers have all
gone. And the works in most cases have disappeared: Wostenholm's
Washington Works, Rodgers' Pond Hill Works, Walker & Hall's
Electro Works, and Richards' and Viner's relatively modern factories
have all been demolished. The edge tool industry suffered in much
the same way as the cutlery industry, and most of the very small
family-run businesses have disappeared, mergers have occurred, the
industry has become highly mechanised and much labour has been
shed.

White's *Sheffield District Directory* for 1893 listed 275 pen, pocket
and sportsmen's knife manufacturers, 281 table knife manufacturers,
97 silver and plated and German silver ware manufacturers, 128
electro-plate and nickel-silver makers, 225 file and rasp
manufacturers, 144 saw manufacturers, 125 scissors manufacturers
and 95 edge tool manufacturers, to name only some of the many
trades then in existence. By contrast in the 2003–04 *Yellow Pages*
directory, there were only forty-five cutlery manufacturers and
wholesalers listed, fourteen electro-platers, fifty-nine toolmakers,
twenty-three manufacturng silversmiths and six saw makers; scissors
makers and file makers were not listed.

The final curtain on Sheffield's longest-existing trades has not
fallen and the good name of Sheffield lives on in the hands of one or
two little mesters and in the names of a handful of cutlery and tool
firms that were first established when Sheffield's light steel trades
ruled the world.

*S*TEEL CITY: THE RISE AND DECLINE OF THE HEAVY STEEL AND ENGINEERING INDUSTRY IN THE LOWER DON VALLEY

6

T he heavy steel and engineering industry was a relative newcomer to Sheffield. It did not emerge on any appreciable scale until the 1850s but by the end of the nineteenth century had overtaken the light steel trades and had resulted in the vast physical expansion of the urban area and explosive population growth.

A new industry in a new location

The new industry was based on the insatiable market that had arisen for machine parts, axles, tyres, boilers and springs for the railways, steel for guns and shells, and plates for ships. And it must be emphasised that the heavy steel industry developed as a branch of the light staple trades of the Sheffield district, not from the expansion of the iron producing plants. There was no integration of the iron and steel industries: the steel making capacity existed where there were no

The geographical separation of the light steel trades and the heavy steel industry in Sheffield as exemplified by scissors making and steel tilting, rolling and forging in 1900. The scissors manufacturers are located in and around the old town, while the heavy steel tilting, rolling and forging plants are overwhelmingly concentrated in the Lower Don Valley. Source of data: White's General and Commercial Directory of Sheffield and Rotherham, 1900

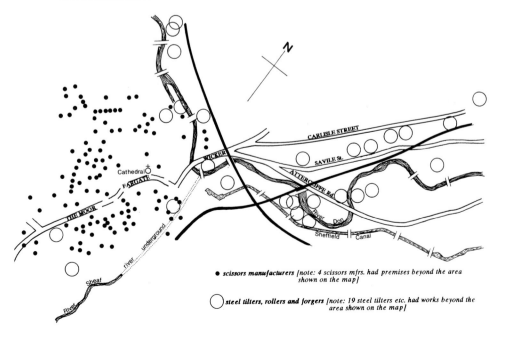

● *scissors manufacturers [note: 4 scissors mfrs. had premises beyond the area shown on the map]*

◯ *steel tilters, rollers and forgers [note: 19 steel tilters etc. had works beyond the area shown on the map]*

blast furnaces. To meet the rapidly growing demand, light steel firms - including what were to become household names late in the century, eg, John Brown (who started as a cutler), Charles Cammell (file maker) and Thomas Firth (file, saw and edge toolmaker) set up new works to manufacture steel on a bigger scale.

Throughout the 1850s, before the adoption of the Bessemer process, the only way of producing the large ingots of high quality steel required by the market was to assemble in one works a large number of converting (cementation) furnaces, crucible holes, and puddling furnaces (for making wrought iron for plate production and puddled steel). This naturally led to the growth of large new steel works. These were mostly built on 'green field' sites in the wide Don valley to the east of the town in Brightside and then Attercliffe. There was flat land beside the river for the construction and subsequent expansion of the large works and in the surrounding area for houses for the workers who were attracted in large numbers. In addition there was a constant supply of water from the River Don and access via the Sheffield and Rotherham railway and its branch lines to the coking coal from local collieries, and to the pig iron from the continent. The new industry also took advantage of good locations beside the Manchester-Sheffield railway to the north-west of

John Brown's Atlas Works established in 1857, a mass of converting furnaces (with their characteristic conical chimneys), crucible shops and puddling furnaces (with their tall smoking chimneys). The engraving dates from 1863.

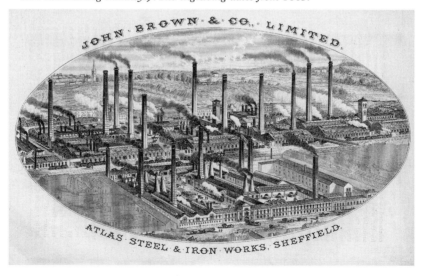

Sheffield in the villages of Owlerton, Wadsley, and Oughtibridge, and even Stocksbridge on the Little Don where Samuel Fox had set up his works in 1841. It has been calculated that the light and heavy steel trades of the Don valley between Stocksbridge in the north-west, round the elbow-bend and through Sheffield, past Rotherham to Swinton, accounted for 80–90 per cent of British steel making capacity in the early 1850s.[1]

The Bessemer converter made its first appearance on Carlisle Street at Bessemer's Steel Works in the very midst of the new steel works, with their many cementation furnaces and crucible holes, in 1858. This was a radical step by its inventor Henry Bessemer

Interior of the Bessemer Steel Works on Carlisle Street as portrayed in Pawson & Brailsford's Illustrated Guide to Sheffield *in 1879. In the vertical Bessemer converter on the left pressurised air is being forced into molten haematite pig iron to remove the non-metallic elements (mainly silicon and iron) resulting in a fantastic firework display. On the right, the 'blowing down' has been completed (it took about half an hour), the air blow turned off, the pig iron has been transformed into mild steel and the converter is tipped on its side to allow the steel to be poured into a ladle carried on a turntable. The ladle was then carried on a crane and the steel teemed into cast iron moulds which when the steel had cooled became ingots ready for the forge or rolling mills. In the left foreground can be seen a workman operating the mechanism that controlled the air blast. Other levers shown shifted the converter from the horizontal to the vertical and to the horizontal again.*

following the sceptical reception of the new invention by the rather conservative (in terms of methods of production if not in terms of business acumen) Sheffield steel producers. The scepticism arose from doubts about the process itself and about the quality of the large amounts of steel that were produced in a short space of time. Using traditional methods of converting pig iron into blister steel and then into crucible steel, took fourteen or fifteen days to produce a 40–50 pound ingot of cast steel, whereas the Bessemer process could produce six tons of cast steel in about thirty minutes. Bessemer, the outsider, saw his new works initially as a place of demonstration for potential licensees who could have their own pig iron converted into Bessemer steel before taking out a licence. Two of Sheffield's major new firms, John Brown's and Charles Cammell's, became the earliest converts and produced their first Bessemer steel rails in 1861, followed by Samuel Fox in 1863.[2]

Large, progressive firms dominated the industry, and did so from its earliest days. The nature of the industry demanded a large amount of capital and large scale mechanised operations, and this led to the concentration of the industry in relatively few hands, in marked contrast to the situation in the light steel trades. By the first decade of the twentieth century there were at least eight firms employing more than 2,000 workers and six firms employing between 1,000 and 2,000 men. Employers were unhampered by strong traditionalist unions, many of the workers being new to the trade – migrants from the surrounding countryside and beyond, including many from Ireland. New methods of production, therefore, were used in the industry from its inception.

The biggest concentration of the heavy steel and engineering industry was in Brightside and Attercliffe – the 'East End' of Sheffield. The beginnings of this massing together of the new industry had been evident in the 1850s but by the beginning of the twentieth century it was no longer a thin and broken line of industrial premises but an almost solid mass of works and railway sidings surrounded by rows of terraced houses. The greatest concentration of works began within half a mile of the city centre along Carlisle Street and Savile Street This complex included Charles Cammell's Cyclops Works, John Brown's Atlas Works (both works appropriately named after giants of Greek mythology), Henry Bessemer's Steel Works and Thomas Firth's Norfolk Works with the railway running beside and between the works.

Writing in the early 1870s Alfred Gatty, in his *Sheffield Past and Present*, described the once rural scene and the dramatic changes that

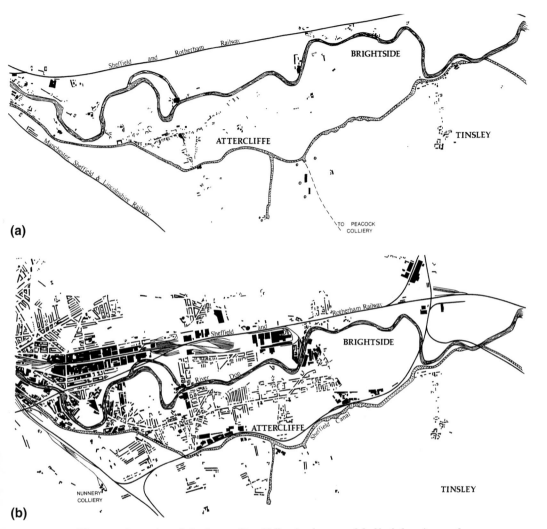

The transformation of the Lower Don Valley in the second half of the nineteenth century: (a) housing and industry in the early 1850s and (b) housing and industry in the 1890s. Source: traced from Ordnance Survey six-inch sheets

had taken place there. He said that in the 1820s the town completely stopped at the Wicker, below Spital Hill. And looking into the Don valley from Osgathorpe, 'the eye traversed a rich and extended scene of agricultural interest and beauty'. An ancient wood, Hall Carr Wood, clothed the hillside above the village of Attercliffe and beyond, the church spire of Laughton en le Morthen and the church tower of

Handsworth 'were distinctly visible through the clear atmosphere with Treeton and Whiston in the intervening distance.' He contrasted this pre-industrial landscape with the one confronting the observer in the early 1870s:

> *The wood has disappeared, cottages have sprung up on the hillside, and down in the valley, where the railway shoots its straight line beside the meandering Don, there stands, as it were, Dante's city of Dis: masses of buildings, from the tops of which issue fire, and smoke, and steam, which cloud the whole scene, however bright the sunshine. But in that once lovely valley, is concentrated the great source of Sheffield prosperity. The work done on the north-east of Sheffield accounts for the luxury enjoyed in the west ...*[3]

Forncett Street, Brightside lying on the slopes to the north of the River Don in close proximity to the steelworks of Henry Bessemer, John Brown (Atlas Works), and Charles Cammell (Norfolk Works). Ordnance Survey, twenty-five inch sheet, 294.04, 1905

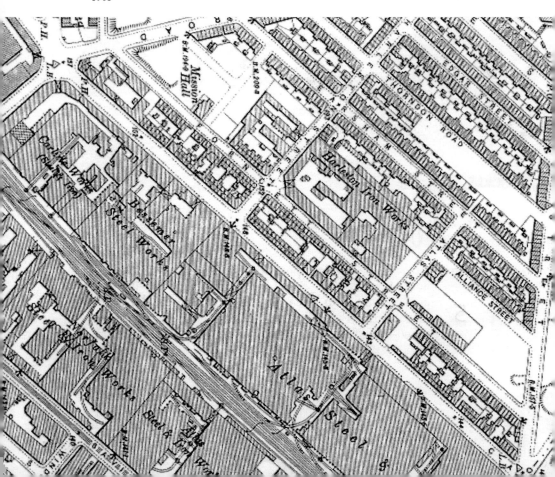

Even though, as alluded to by Gatty in the quotation above, the factory owners lived in their villas in Ecclesall and Ranmoor, the new steel works attracted to the east end of Sheffield a rapidly growing population. Brightside's population trebled between 1841 and 1861 (from 10,089 to 29,818), doubled by 1881 (to 56,719) and had reached 75,000 by the end of the century. Attercliffe's population growth was not quite on the same scale but still impressive: from 4,156 in 1841 to 7,464 in 1861 then a giant leap to nearly 30,000 in 1881 and to nearly 52,000 in 1901. And a great number of the new residents of Brightside and Attercliffe, and Burngreave, Grimesthorpe and Darnall were in-migrants from near and far. For example, a study of the inhabitants aged fourteen years and over living in ninety-four houses in Forncett Street in 1871 within a stone's throw of three important steel works belonging to Henry Bessemer, John Brown and Charles Cammell showed that eighty-five per cent (408 out of 449) were migrants. There were more people living in Forncett Street from Staffordshire (forty-two) than from Sheffield, and more people from Ireland (fifty-one) than from any county in England and Wales. Nearly a half of the inhabitants of Forncett Street originated more than fifty miles from Sheffield.[4]

A change of emphasis

The *raison d'être* of the establishment of the heavy steel industry in the 1850s was, as has already been pointed out, the demand for rails, tyres and axles for the railways and plates for ships for the British navy. By 1900 there had been a change of emphasis: special steels, armaments and heavy engineering had almost completely taken the place of railway products and only three local plants, none of them in Sheffield's east end, continued to make rails – Cammell's at Penistone, Samuel Fox at Stocksbridge and Steel, Peech and Tozer at Rotherham.

After the re-equipment of the railways in Britain with steel rails, rail manufacture tended to move to the coasts from were overseas markets could be more easily served. Although the unfavourable locational circumstances checked the production of common-grade steel in Sheffield, they did not check the development of the industry. They merely diverted development into new channels, namely the production of steels where the cost of manufacture and the value of the product far exceeded the cost of raw material assembly and distribution, and in whose making, scrap could be extensively used.

Specialisation became the keynote of the heavy trades and the research laboratory became an important factor in the Sheffield

Armour plate rolling at John Brown's Atlas Works. Sheffield and Neighbourhood, Pawson & Brailsford, 1889

steel industry after 1880. Almost immediately the research bore fruit and in 1883 Robert Hadfield patented his non-magnetic manganese steel which was used for tramway and railway points and crossings and accelerated the growth of the electrical industries. And his 'Era' steel possessed remarkable resistance to the impact of projectiles and was used in the most vulnerable parts on warships such as conning towers and ammunition and communication tubes. The firm also manufactured millions of shells of every size and description.

The most famous names in the industry also increasingly concentrated on armament production: John Brown's and Cammell's increasingly specialising in the manufacture of armour plate, and Firth's on gun barrels and armour piercing shells. Before the First World War Sheffield was 'the greatest Armoury the world has ever seen'.[5] Other firms also increasingly concentrated production on specialised products. For example, Samuel Osborn's specialised in cast steel 'of every description from a few ounces to 15 Tons each' and were the sole manufacturers of Mushet's 'special steel' and 'titanic steel' used in the manufacture of specialised tools, drills and dies. Jessop's specialised in cast steel for engineering, machinery and edge tool purposes, Jonas & Colver's specialised in steel for small

Advertisement for Wm Jessop's Brightside Works. White's Sheffield District Directory, 1893

arms manufacture; and W T Beesley manufactured steel to a quarter of a thousandth of an inch in exactness.

The larger firms also acquired interests outside Sheffield by the beginning of the twentieth century. Cammell's, for example, besides having two steel plants in Sheffield, had another steel works at Penistone, ironworks at Workington and Maryport in Cumberland, shipyards at Birkenhead, haematite iron mines in Cumberland, and New Oaks Colliery at Barnsley. John Brown's (which had partially amalgamated with Firth's in 1904), had shipyards on the Clyde, iron mines in Northamptonshire and in Spain and collieries in South Yorkshire. Vickers had a shipyard at Barrow. In 1910 it was claimed that all three firms were capable of 'turning out a battleship complete'.[6]

By the beginning of the First World War, in spite of the steady expansion of the light steel trades, the heavy steel trades dominated industry in Sheffield. While its sister industry had expanded slowly and unevenly, the heavy steel industry had gone forward by leaps and bounds. The industry employed about 40,000 workers in 1914, an increase of 80 per cent since 1891. Between 1891–1911, employment in steel making had increased by 50 per cent and in engineering by more than 80 per cent. There were 193 firms in the city engaged in refining and manufacturing steel, 41 firms engaged in rolling and forging steel and there were 33 foundries.

Wartime conditions, depression, and boom
In the First World War production was at a very high level with the Ministry of Munitions co-ordinating production levels and types of specialisation. Many new workers, many of them in-migrants joined the labour force and were housed in 'munitions huts' scattered throughout the Don valley. Many women for the first time worked in the steel industry in the East End. And the industry itself was modernised to meet the wartime needs for armaments and was equipped with 'modern shops, modern methods and resources of output almost double those of pre-war days'[7] and provided markets could be found in the peace time conditions following the end of hostilities the industry was well equipped to provide steel for every purpose.

Following the end of the war there was a short boom. In this period the progressive firms, sought and supplied new markets to replace the old ones: China, Japan, Australia, Canada and the British colonies now loomed much larger overseas and the new aircraft and motor car industries provided new outlets for special steels. But the boom did not last and it was over by late 1920.

Turning heavy shells at Cammell Laird's Norfolk Works during the First World War.
Author's postcard collection

From then until the re-armament of the Army, the Royal Navy and Royal Air Force, in the second half of the 1930s there was mass unemployment in Sheffield and the heavy steel and engineering industry suffered badly. In the middle of October 1920 there were less than 6,000 unemployed workers in the city but within a week this had more than doubled to 13,000 and a year later the figure had risen to between 40,000 and 50,000. After that date over the next decade there were periods of marked improvement but also major setbacks and between May and September 1932 unemployment in the city was between 60,000 and 70,000 out of a total workforce of 171,000 – a staggering figure of between 35 and 41 per cent. It has been estimated that employment in Sheffield's heavy trades decreased from 66,000 in 1921 to 47,000 in 1931 – a fall of nearly 29 per cent.[8]

But technical change went on in this period of recession and depression. The electric arc furnace, which had been introduced just before the outbreak of the First World War became increasingly important in the production of special steels, output from electric arc furnaces rising from 55,000 tons of ingots and castings in 1920 to 221,000 tons in 1939 – more than three-quarters of total British electric arc production. Electric crucibles also slowly took over from the coke-fired crucible from the late 1920s. Increasing mechanisation went on throughout the industry.

Structural re-organisation was also a feature of the inter-war period, in the form of amalgamations followed by much-needed rationalisation. Although just beyond the boundaries of Sheffield in neighbouring Rotherham, steel makers Steel, Peech & Tozer and Samuel Fox of Stocksbridge amalgamated in 1918 to form the United Steel Companies Ltd and acquired the Frodingham Iron & Steel Co Ltd (to provide a cheap source of Lincolnshire pig iron and to stifle regional competition), Rothervale Collieries (Treeton, Orgreave and Thurcroft) and Workington Iron & Steel Co Ltd. In its heyday this combine was the largest producer of steel in the British Empire.[9] In 1928 another important amalgamation took place, that of Vickers and Cammell-Laird to form the English Steel Corporation, resulting in the modernisation of Cammell's Grimesthorpe Works and Vickers' River Don Works in the lower Don valley. Then in 1930 Thomas Firth & Sons and John Brown, which had been working closely together since the beginning of the century, formally merged to form Firth-Brown's. Of the five giants of Sheffield's east end, only Hadfield's remained an independent firm on the outbreak of the Second World War.

With the onset of war in 1939, after two decades of peace but also mostly of difficult and depressed trading, production again reached full capacity and was turned over almost entirely to the production of war materials. And despite the withering bomb attacks on the city in December 1940, the heavy steel works escaped relatively unscathed. And they made a massive contribution to the war effort.[10] At the Vickers River Don Works in the first eighteen months of the war was the only drop hammer in the country capable of forging Spitfire crankshafts. The English Steel Corporation's factories also supplied armour plating for the country's fighter planes and tanks and side and deck armour for the Navy's battleships, besides gun barrels of every size and the 'Grand Slam' bomb. A similar story can be told of the work of another great combine, the United Steel Companies Ltd. At their Stocksbridge Works, for example, they specialised in the production of alloy steels, mainly for aircraft production. They also produced springs in large quantities for service vehicles and tanks and for Bren and Bofors guns. The wire products made at the Stocksbridge Works were also in great demand for motor and aero engines and for precision instruments. The umbrella department went over full time to the production of cartridge clips for Browning automatic guns. The war production of Firth Brown was also immense, making more than a million tons of high quality alloy steel, large amounts of armour for battleships, carriers, cruisers and tanks, and 360,000 bombs and shells. It was said that they could produce 'shells to go through any armour and armour to resist any shell'.[11] The other giant firm, Hadfield's, employed more than 10,000 workers during the war years and among their products were more than $4^1/_2$ million shells and bombs, either completely finished or as forgings or castings, more than a million armour plates for aircraft, and no less than three million tank track shoes in silico-manganese steel. The story is almost endless with the smaller firms making major contributions from Darwin's making heavy magnets for use in minesweepers to counteract the magnetic mine, and Tinsley Wire Industries making anti-torpedo nets, to Craven's, the railway carriage and wagon builders, building airframes for the Lysander reconnaissance aircraft and the Horsa glider, Osborn's making the

Casting 22,000-pound 'Grand Slam' bombs at the Vickers Works of the English Steel Corporation during the Second World War. Drawing by Bob Warburton

steel hinges for the famous Bailey bridges used at river crossings where existing bridges had been destroyed and Newton Chambers making more than 1,000 Churchill tanks at Thorncliffe Ironworks.

Employment shrinkage

In the immediate post-war period stretching into the 1950s and 1960s Sheffield's heavy steel and engineering industry remained in full production, profits were large and there were even labour shortages. The period also saw the giant combines nationalised by the Labour government in 1949, de-nationalised by the Conservatives between 1953 and 1955 and re-nationalised by the Labour in 1967. Through all this boom and structural upheaval, modernisation of the industry continued, most notably in the form of the English Steel Corporation's £26 million Tinsley Park Works that opened in 1963, and Sheffield remained a major steel producer, most importantly for alloy steels for the engineering industry.

But drastic change and decline were just over the horizon. Despite the opening of English Steel's Shepcote Lane stainless plant, the biggest in Europe, in 1976, the decade saw the loss of home markets through the shrinkage in its domestic industrial customers in the shipbuilding, car and aircraft industries and overseas markets were

Sheffield Forgemasters, an almost lone traditional presence in the fast-changing landscape of the Lower Don Valley. Joan Jones

continually shrunk through high exchange rates and tough competition not only from its European and North American rivals but also from Third World competitors such as Brazil and South Korea where labour costs were much lower. Further mergers and rationalisation were the result: the ESC's Tinsley Park works was closed and removed; Hadfield's, now Dunford Hadfield's, took over Osborn's and Brown Bayleys, and the nationalised British Steel Corporation entered into joint activities called 'Phoenix', with private firms.

But this did not halt the industry's rapid decline that became most severe in the late 1970s and early 1980s. In spite of a bitter national strike in 1981, large plant after large plant was closed and eventually swept away. John Brown's Atlas Works opened in 1857 was closed in 1983 and Hadfield's massive East Hecla Works opened in 1898 was closed in the same year. Employment in the lower Don valley declined from 40,000 in the mid-seventies

Two reminders of the past: the five ton steam hammer built by Brightside Engineering Company in 1947, the thump of which would have been heard day and night standing at the junction of Savile Street East and Sutherland Street; and the former entrance to Thomas Firth's Siemens Department on Savile Street. Joan Jones

to 13,000 in just over ten years; most of the residential population had already been re-housed elsewhere and nearly half the land in the valley was either cleared, semi-derelict or contained empty works. Sheffield Forgemasters, created from the merging of some of the most ancient names in the industry, managed to keep its head above water and managed to prosper. But in large parts of the valley the green field sites of a century and a quarter earlier had now become brown field sites. The city was in shock and the lower Don valley was badly in need of economic and environmental regeneration.[12]

7 *E*MINENT SHEFFIELD VICTORIANS

During Victoria's reign, from 1837 to 1901, the town, then city of Sheffield, grew enormously in population, physical size and industrial importance. During the period a galaxy of men and women, both natives and long-term residents who were born elsewhere, rose to local, national or international prominence in their chosen field. Some of them also left their mark on the place because they were important benefactors. At no time, before or since, has Sheffield produced or attracted to live and work here such a cast of eminent people across such a broad spectrum of activity. Obviously successful industrialists loom large in any such list, but the selective list of eminent Victorians whose lives are discussed in this chapter also includes scientists, engineers, musicians, architects, artists, poets, historians and children's writers.

Captains of industry

The not surprisingly long list of successful industrialists is an interesting mixture of the native-born and incomers. The two greatest Victorian cutlery magnates, John Rodgers and George Wostenholm, were both native-born. **John Rodgers** (1779–1859) followed his grandfather and father, both Joseph Rodgers, to be head of the firm

of Joseph Rodgers and Sons, the leading cutlery firm in Sheffield and – for much of the nineteenth century – in the world, with its famous double mark of a star and Maltese cross which was granted by the Company of Cutlers

George Wostenholm (1800–1876) photographed in New York in 1856, the year he became Master Cutler. Sheffield City Libraries, Local Studies Library

in 1764. Under John Rodgers' leadership the firm rapidly expanded its market throughout Britain (with Rodgers before his father's death in1821 acting as chief salesman and visiting prospective buyers around the country on horseback) and most significantly in the United States. In 1821 John Rodgers was introduced to the Prince Regent and presented him with a tiny knife containing 57 blades and in return the Prince Regent presented the firm with a Royal Warrant. For John Rodgers quality came first and marketing a close second: shortly after the meeting with the Prince Regent he opened the world's first cutlery showroom at the Norfolk Street Works.

Closely following on the heels of Joseph Rodgers and Sons as the major Sheffield cutlery firm in the nineteenth century was the firm of George Wostenholm & Son very ably led by **George Wostenholm** (1800–1876). After serving an apprenticeship with his father (who died in 1833) he was brought into the firm which was then named George Wostenholme & Son (the final 'e' was said to have been subsequently omitted to get the full name on knives). In 1826 George Wostenholm became a freeman of the Company of Cutlers and was granted what was to become his famous trademark **I*XL** (I excel). A combination of long unremitting work hours, outstanding sales skills, and exacting demands on his employees pushed his firm onwards and upwards, based on quality products largely aimed at the American market – razors and a wide range of pocket knives – working knives for farm and frontier with acid-etchings pandering to the American taste and with ivory and pearl handles, and of course Bowie knives in very large numbers. He made thirty transatlantic crossings to secure American orders, sometimes travelling from coast to coast, and in 1848 he bought a works in Wellington Street which was extended and renamed the Washington Works, to mark his strong association with the United States. By the 1860s the Washington Works employed between 600 and 700 workers.

He invested a part of the fortune he amassed in the building of a fine house, Kenwood, at the Sharrow end of Nether Edge, which still stands today as the Kenwood Hotel. The house was designed by William Flockton (see below) and the surrounding park is thought to have been designed by Robert Marnock[1], the designer of Sheffield Botanical Gardens, who may also have had a hand in designing the surrounding 150 acres of farmland on Wostenholm's behalf as a garden suburb. The area was laid out with curving, tree-lined streets and grand stone houses (many built by William Steade hence Steade Road) in a style he had seen and admired in the Eastern United States. Although he married three times he had no children and sold

Mappin Art Gallery. Sheffield and Neighbourhood, Pawson & Brailsford, 1889

the firm to his business partners in 1875 when it became a limited liability company. He left an enormous fortune of a quarter of a million pounds.

Equally swift in their rise to business success and large fortunes were members of the Mappin family, **John Newton Mappin** (d 1884) and **Sir Frederick Thorpe Mappin** (1821–1910). It was John Newton Mappin, a successful brewer who left money in his will for the building of the Mappin Art Gallery and who also bequeathed more than 150 pictures to the gallery. His nephew was Frederick Thorpe Mappin who succeeded his father in 1841 as head of a firm which manufactured a variety of knives and razors. He had joined his father at the early age of fourteen as partner and on his father's death he also took charge of his three younger brothers who were also introduced to the business, the firm being renamed Mappin Brothers in 1851. Like George Wostenholm, Frederick Mappin was an indefatigable traveller on behalf of the firm, within a few years opening a shop and then a warehouse in London and travelling extensively in Europe and North America. At the beginning of the 1850s the firm opened a new factory, the Queen's Works, on Flat Street at the southern end of Fitzalan Square where in the 1850s they employed about 500 workers. However, disputes began to emerge among the Mappin brothers and Frederick left the firm in 1859, which continued to operate under two of the remaining brothers. The third brother, John Newton Mappin, had left the firm to form his own cutlery and silver plate firm which became known as Mappin & Webb. It still exists today and is owned by Asprey & Co, the London jewellers.

On leaving Mappin Brothers, Frederick Mappin became a senior partner in the steel making and engineering firm of Thomas Turton & Sons, was chairman for many years of the Sheffield Gas Company and a director of the Midland Railway. He was Master Cutler in 1855–56, Mayor of Sheffield 1877–78 and Liberal MP for Bassetlaw from 1880 to 1885 and for Hallamshire from 1885 to 1905. He was created a baronet in 1886. He was a generous benefactor to the fledgling University of Sheffield and was made senior pro-chancellor. He left the enormous fortune of nearly £1m.

By the 1870s another group of Sheffield steel manufacturers, this time in the heavy industry, had taken over from the cutlers and silver plate manufacturers as the leading businessmen and, in some cases, political figures in the town, a group headed by **Sir John Brown** (1816–1896). John Brown was the son of a slater born in a courtyard off Fargate in the centre of the town. He rejected his father's

recommendation that he become a linen draper and started his working life as a cutler, then became a steel merchant and finally a steel manufacturer. He made his first fortune through his invention of the steel buffer spring for railway wagons, which was later incorporated into his coat of arms. In 1857 he moved from his works in the town to his new Atlas Works on Carlisle Street to manufacture on a large scale railway components – springs, tyres, axles, wheels and, most

Sir John Brown (1816–1896). Sheffield City Libraries, Local Studies Library

importantly, rails – and rolled wrought iron and steel plate for the Royal Navy's warships. As already pointed out in Chapter 6 John Brown & Co was one of the very first firms to manufacture rails using the Bessemer process.

He moved from his comfortable home at Shirle Hill (where he had entertained the Prime Minister, Lord Palmerston in 1862 and the Lords of the Admiralty in 1863) in 1865 into his newly built Endcliffe Hall set in forty acres of grounds and on which he is reputed to have spent £100,000 to build it and a further £60,000 to furnish it.[2] He was knighted in 1867. He was also active in civic affairs holding the posts of Master Cutler (in 1865 and 1866), Mayor (in 1861 and 1862), Deputy Lieutenant of the West Riding and Chairman of Sheffield School Board.

The opening of Firth Park in 1875. The Graphic. ***Inset: Mark Firth (1819–1880)***.
Sheffield City Libraries, Local Studies Library

Not quite as important as a manufacturer as Sir John Brown, but as a benefactor with few equals was **Mark Firth** (1819–80). Mark was the son of Thomas Firth who had moved to Sheffield from Pontefract and became head melter for Sanderson's, crucible steel manufacturers. Mark's first job was as a clerk at Sanderson's but in 1846, his father together with Mark and Mark's four brothers founded their own firm making crucible steel for axes, saws, files and later railway locomotive and carriage springs. In the early 1850s in order to expand they re-sited their works on Savile Street (the Norfolk Works). In the early 1860s they expanded their new works by building a gun works. Although still manufacturing files, saws and edge tools they increasingly concentrated on ordnance steel, shell steel, steel for rifle barrels and large castings for marine and other engines.

Mark Firth became a wealthy man and eventually left his Wilkinson Street home for Ranmoor where be bought twenty-six acres of land in which he built a mansion, Oakbrook. Like John Brown he rose to

Jessop Hospital for Women in Gell Street. Sheffield and Neighbourhood, Pawson & Brailsford, 1889

become Master Cutler (in 1867, 1868 and 1869) and Mayor (in 1875). His gifts to the town were of immense value. He helped to fund the building of Methodist chapels, funded the building of almshouses at Hanging Water, founded Firth College, the forerunner of the University of Sheffield, and provided Firth Park for the town in 1875, carved out of his Page Hall estate.

Equally philanthropic were steel manufacturers **Thomas Jessop** (1804–1887) and **William Edgar Allen** (1838–1915) and **Samuel Fox** (1815–1887). Thomas Jessop was born in Blast Lane in Sheffield Park and joined his father, William Jessop, in their expanding steel firm of William Jessop & Son which was located in premises next to their home in Blast Lane. It soon moved to Brightside and later another plant was opened at Kilnhurst, north of Rotherham. Thomas Jessop rose quickly in importance and he was elected Mayor of Sheffield and Master Cutler in 1863, a double honour in the same year not repeated before or since. As his fortune increased he moved house several times, at one point he lived at Claremont, later a private hospital, then Shirle Hill, formerly the home of Sir John Brown, and finally Endcliffe Grange, where he died. After the Sheffield Flood of 1864 he was responsible for raising the funds for the relief of the families affected by the disaster. He will be best remembered for providing nearly £30,000 for the building, furnishing and equipping of the Jessop Hospital for Women, opened in Gell Street in 1878.

William Edgar Allen was also born in Sheffield. He was an accomplished linguist who used his skills early on in his career as a foreign traveller for Ibbotson Brothers, cutlers of the Globe Works. He founded his own firm at the Imperial Steel Works in 1867. He gave substantial sums to a number of deserving causes but will be best remembered for providing the Edgar Allen Library at the University of Sheffield and the Edgar Allen Institute for Medico-Mechanical Treatment.

Samuel Fox was born in Bradwell, Derbyshire, the youngest of eight children. His father was a weavers' shuttle maker. Samuel chose wire drawing as his career and he was apprenticed to Cocker Brothers who had a mill in Hathersage, and later went to work for them in Sheffield but left because he wanted to set up in business himself. Using capital from the sale of land left to him in his father's will he first went into partnership at a water-powered mill in the Rivelin valley but soon decided to go it alone and leased another water-powered site in the Little Don valley just above Stock's Bridge, which was just that, a stone bridge across the river. There was no village and the area was completely rural. But his business went from strength to strength. To start with Fox manufactured steel wire (for carding in the wool textile industry) and various kinds of pins. But he had a keen eye for the market and began to make crinoline wire and umbrella frames. It is said that sales of his Paragon umbrella frame brought him his first fortune of half a million pounds.. In the late 1850s and early 1860s he extended his Stocksbridge Works in order to be independent of his steel suppliers and to take advantage of the latest technology. In 1862 he installed two Bessemer converters, a cogging mill and a rolling mill. He had entered the bulk steel trade and steel rails for the railways brought him his second fortune. He died in 1887 and was a substantial benefactor not only in Stocksbridge but also in his native Bradwell in the form of workers' housing in Stocksbridge and contributions to the upkeep of schools, churches and chapels and the establishment of charities in both places.

Two other great Victorian Sheffield industrialists were **Edward Vickers** (1804–1897) and **Charles Cammell** (*c.*1809–1879). Sheffield-born Edward Vickers took over the steel firm Naylor, Vickers & Co from his brother and as expansion took place, moved the business from the old Don Steel Works at Millsands in 1867 to the newly-built new Don Steel Works in Brightside. He was Mayor of Sheffield in 1847 and a JP for many years. He lived for many years at Tapton Hall which he built in 1853, before retiring to Oxfordshire. His son, **Thomas Edward Vickers** (1833–1915) took over on his father's retirement and was elected Master Cutler in 1872 and later was awarded the honour of the Companionship of the Order of Bath.

Charles Cammell was a native of Hull who came to Sheffield as a young man with just a few pounds in his pocket and, like William Edgar Allen, worked for some years as a traveller for Ibbotson Brothers. He then co-founded a firm called Johnson, Cammell & Co manufacturing edge tools and files. The business did well, and became, as Charles Cammell & Co, a major manufacturer of steel components for the railways and later munitions, moving to the Cyclops Works in Savile Street as early as 1845, thus setting the trend for the industrialisation of the lower Don valley. In 1851 he bought Norton Hall and became 'squire' of Norton, dying there in 1879.

Scientists and engineers

The continued success of Sheffield's steel-based industries in the late nineteenth and early twentieth centuries owed almost as much to scientific research as business skill and the work of Brearley (see Chapter 5), Hadfield and Sorby was outstanding.

Sir Robert Hadfield (1858–1940). Sheffield City Libraries, Local Studies Library

Sir Robert Abbott Hadfield (1858–1940), had the distinction of not only being a successful industrialist but also a brilliant applied scientist. Attercliffe-born, Hadfield was the son of Robert Hadfield who had moved from a career as a rate collector with the Board of Guardians into the steel industry and set up a business in 1872 that manufactured steel castings at the Hecla Works in Newhall Road. The young Hadfield was educated at the Collegiate School and then worked for a short period for Jonas and Colver, manufacturers of cast steel for tools, saws and files, before joining his father's firm. In 1883, at the age of only twenty-five, he took out his first patent for non-magnetic manganese steel. This was followed in 1884 with his discovery of silicon steel and various other alloy steels followed. On his father's death he became chairman of the firm and in 1898 opened a new works, the East Hecla Works, devoted almost entirely to the production of armaments, on the site now largely occupied by the Meadowhall shopping centre. He was Master Cutler in 1899, was knighted by King Edward VII in 1908 and elected a Fellow of the Royal Society in 1909.

Rather more unsung, locally at any rate, throughout most of his life, was **Dr Henry Clifton Sorby** (1826–1908) who came from a long-standing Sheffield family that provided the first Master Cutler (Robert Sorby) in 1624. Sorby was of independent means and did not need to work for a living, but this modest and learned man dedicated his life to scientific research and, rather than become a member of one of the leading universities, he chose to live his life in Sheffield. His interests and achievements were far-ranging. The Geological Society hailed him as 'The Father of Microscopic Petrology' (the microscopic study of the composition of rocks); and more importantly for Sheffield industry he pioneered the new science of metallography, the microscopic structure and properties of metals. He was also an expert on meteorology, the composition of meteorites, the nature of colouring in hair, flowers, minerals and birds' eggs, the detection of poisons, aspects of Egyptology, and the materials used in Roman, Saxon and Norman architecture. He was a Fellow of the Geological Society and of the prestigious Royal Society. He supported the University of Sheffield during its formative years and endowed a Chair of Geology. The Sorby Natural History Society is named after him.

Two of the country's great Victorian railway engineers, Joseph Locke and Sir John Fowler, were born in the Sheffield area, but Joseph Locke, went to live in Barnsley when he was five and really does not qualify for this list.

Sir John Fowler (1817–1898) was the child of John and Elizabeth Fowler of Wadsley Hall. John senior was an estate valuer and surveyor who has a fine monument in Sheffield General Cemetery. Young John Fowler was educated at John Rider's boarding school at Whitley Hall between Grenoside and Ecclesfield. He left school at sixteen and became a pupil engineer of Mr Towlerton Leather at Sheffield Waterworks. In this capacity he received a good training in waterworks engineering and he became responsible for the

The Forth Bridge under construction.

superintendence of Rivelin and Crookes reservoirs. From time to time he was sent to Leeds to assist Mr Leather's uncle who was engineer on the Aire and Calder Navigation. He then helped to survey a possible route in the upper Don valley for a railway between Sheffield and Manchester. He also spent two years in London with the railway engineer J W Rastrick and then became resident engineer on the Stockton to Darlington Railway.

He became an independent consultant railway engineer in 1844 when he was still only twenty-six years of age and in this capacity he held the position of chief engineer of the Midland Railway. In the early 1860s he was chief engineer on the construction of one of the earliest of London's underground railways, the Metropolitan Railway.[3] He was later involved in the extension of the underground at deeper levels beneath London. He was also closely involved with the building of the Victoria and Pimlico railway bridges, the Sheffield to Grimsby railway, the London to Brighton line, and Millwall Docks. He was also involved in railway engineering schemes in Egypt, India and Norway. In 1866 he was elected President of the Institution of Mechanical Engineers.

His greatest achievement, however, with his partner Sir Benjamin Baker, was the Forth railway bridge in Scotland, completed in 1890. The bridge is one and a half miles long, 300 feet high, cost £3^1/$_2$ m and at the time of its construction was called one of the seven wonders of the modern world. He was made a baronet by Queen Victoria in 1885.[4]

The literary elite

Sheffield's most influential writer – at least the most influential for those wanting to know about Sheffield and the surrounding area in the distant past – was not a novelist or poet but a historian. He wrote monumental works about Sheffield and the rest of South Yorkshire, but only after he had left Sheffield for good. The **Revd Joseph Hunter** (1783–1861) was born in Sheffield, the son of Michael Hunter, a cutler. Previous generations of the family had lived at Hatfield House just inside Ecclesfield parish. His mother died when he was young and he was placed under the guardianship of and brought up by the Revd Joseph Evans, who was minister at the Upper Chapel in the town and then of a Presbyterian church. Hunter received a rudimentary classical education at Mr Sorsby's school in Attercliffe and then in 1806 went to study at the Presbyterian College at York. In 1809 Hunter was appointed minister at Trim Street Chapel in Bath when fashionable 'Regency Bath' was at its height. He remained there until the early 1830s, having married a local doctor's daughter in 1815 with whom he had six children. Shortly after the publication of his second major work on South Yorkshire he left Bath for London where in 1833 he was appointed a sub-Commissioner of Public Records. In 1838 he became Assistant Keeper, First Class in the newly established Public Record Office. There he played a major role for over twenty years in arranging and calendaring records and editing record publications. His output of published work was prodigious, covering a wide range of historical, archaeological and literary interests. He died in London on 9 May 1861 but the body of this 'gentleman of the old school'[5] was brought from his Torrington Square home to Ecclesfield churchyard where he was buried on 15 May by Dr Alfred Gatty in a plot that he had himself selected on a visit to the vicarage a few months previously under 'the waving shadows of some ancient willows.'[6]

Hunter's three major works on South Yorkshire were all published after he had left Sheffield for good and settled into his pastoral duties in Somerset. He is quoted as saying that his interest in antiquarian studies began when he was young and were 'among the amusements of childhood and the chief pleasures of youth' and he is known to have been an assiduous visitor on horseback to all corners of South Yorkshire in pursuit of his studies. His 'Church Notes' on South Yorkshire, compiled in 1801–02 when he was only eighteen or nineteen years are in the British Museum. He took with him to Bath many of the assiduously collected raw materials for his later publications. He published his *Hallamshire* – full title *Hallamshire. The History and Topography of the Parish of Sheffield, in the County of York, with Historical and Descriptive Notes of the Parishes of Ecclesfield, Hansworth, Treaton and Whiston, and the Chapelry of Bradfield* – in 1819. This was followed by *South Yorkshire: The History and Topography of the Deanery of Doncaster in the Diocese and County*

Joseph Hunter (1783–1861).

of York in two volumes in 1828 and 1831. In the short interval between these two volumes he published (in 1829) *The Hallamshire Glossary*, a dictionary of the regional dialect of the Sheffield area. No one doing work on the history of the Sheffield area can avoid making use of Hunter's *Hallamshire* and no one working on the history of any South Yorkshire parish or village can afford to ignore Hunter's *South Yorkshire*. The family trees of prominent families are also important features of his *South Yorkshire* – there are 104 in Volume 1 and 123 in Volume 2.

Hunter's *Hallamshire Glossary* is a pioneering work, being among a group of about half a dozen early works on regional dialect when its study was in its infancy.[7] He records formally for the first time South Yorkshire dialect words and local pronunciations that are still with us today.

Alfred Gatty, who after Hunter's death revised, edited and re-published Hunter's *Hallamshire*, was of the opinion that Hunter 'stands second to none amongst the names which do honour to Sheffield as a birth-place'.[8]

Another local writer who lived a life quite different from Hunter's was the poet **Ebenezer Elliott** (1781–1849). Elliott was born in Masbrough, now part of Rotherham, but he lived in Sheffield for twenty-two years, living from 1819 to 1834 in Burgess Street off Barker's Pool and from 1834 to 1841 in Upperthorpe in the house built by the Master Cutler John Blake who had died of cholera in 1832. After Elliott's death the citizens of Sheffield and Rotherham subscribed £600 for the erection in 1854 of a bronze statue on a granite plinth to the man, that stood in the Market Place before being moved in 1875 to Weston Park, where it remains to this day.[9]

Elliott's character must have been strongly influenced by his father, an enterprising, outspoken man with deeply held political and religious convictions and strong literary interests, who eventually owned the New Foundry in Masbrough and an ironmonger's shop in Rotherham High Street. Elliott was one of eleven children born to Ebenezer Elliott senior and his wife Ann. He caught smallpox when he was three and this left him with a pock-marked face for the rest of his life. He was educated at a number of local schools, where he was thoroughly miserable and believed he had learned next to nothing, until he was sixteen, when, much to his relief, he was sent to work in his father's iron foundry, in which he became a partner (probably on his marriage in 1806), and then took over the firm from his father and brother before going bankrupt in 1816. In 1819, with the help of a loan of £100 from his two sisters-in-law, he moved to Sheffield and

Ebenezer Elliott (1783–1849).
John Guest, Historic Notices of Rotherham, 1879

set up a new business as an iron and steel merchant, which by the 1830s had been enlarged to become a steel manufacturing firm.

As a young man, outside of work he attended chapel and later took to frequent visits to local public houses. He is said to have had no literary interests until he visited his aunt and happened to see a cousin's book on botany and then heard his brother reciting a poem about flowering plants. These ignited his interest in natural history and the world of books. He became a lover of nature and the local countryside and an avid reader of poetry, gothic novels and books on topography and travel which formed the basis of his early verse about seducers and cruelly deceived maidens.

This subject matter was dropped after 1815 with the passing of the corn laws which were not repealed until 1846. The corn laws or the 'Bread Tax' as Elliott called them, were passed by a government made up principally of landowners and were designed to restrict grain imports, and therefore keep the price of home-grown grain artificially high. This resulted in good profits for landowners from their home farms and from farm tenants' rents while driving up the price of bread. To Elliott the corn laws not only interfered with free trade, they greatly increased the possibility of famine, and reduced the demand for manufactured goods at home and abroad, and therefore increased the possibility of widespread unemployment. His crusade was for working men and industrialists against the idle rich and parasites, referring to the latter as 'Lord Pauper' and 'Squire Leech'. He attacked the laws unremittingly for over a quarter of a century through lectures, poems, hymns and the press, and became a household name. Elliott was a small, mild-mannered man who was raised to a state of almost apoplectic wrath on the subject of the corn laws. He did not believe in physical revolution (he resigned from the Chartist movement because they were embracing physical violence);

he believed the world could be changed through education, hard work, the love of nature, dialogue between the classes and, of course, the repeal of the corn laws. His motto was one word: 'Right'. He often signed himself 'Ebenezer Elliott, C. L. R.[Corn Law Rhymer]'.

Elliott left Sheffield for health reasons in 1841 and went to live in retirement at Hargate Hill in Great Houghton. He lived there until his death in 1849, aged 68, enjoying a quiet life, continuing his literary pursuits and at first enjoying the country life but later regretting his move. He is buried in Darfield churchyard.

Elliott was more than a polemicist. His love of nature and local scenery inspired a series of poems in praise of the local landscape about such places as Rivelin, Roche Abbey, Win Hill, Wincobank Hill and the rivers Don and Rother. In 'To the Don and Rother', for example, he looks back to the days of his childhood in Masbrough:

When in my mother's arms, an infant frail,
Along your windings borne,
My blue eyes caught your glimmer in the vale,
And halcyons darted o'er your willows pale
On wings like morn.

Even in his political verses his characters find time to, or are exalted to, commune with nature or wonder at the beauty of the local scene as in 'The Ranter':

Up, sluggards, up! And drink the morning breeze,
The birds on cloud-left Osgathorpe awake;
And Wincobank is waving all his trees
O-er subject towns, and farms and villages,
And gleaming streams, and woods, and waterfalls.

The countryside and natural history also provided a major stimulus to **Mrs Margaret Gatty** (1809–1873) and her daughter **Juliana** (1841–1885), better known under her married name of **Mrs Ewing**.[10]

Margaret Gatty was the wife of **Dr Alfred Gatty** (1813–1903) who deserves a paragraph in his own right. Gatty was a Londoner and educated at Charterhouse, Eton and Oxford where he was sent down before receiving his degree for being implicated in the death of a man knocked down by a rowdy party of students. After six months he returned to college for a term and was received into holy orders by the Bishop of Ripon in 1837 and then spent two years as curate of

Bellerby in the parish of Spennithorne in the then North Riding. Because his church had no cemetery or licence for conducting the marriage service he 'never buried a corpse or married a couple',[11] but what he did do was to meet his future wife, who was the daughter of the Revd Alexander John Scott, Lord Nelson's former chaplain, foreign secretary and intelligence officer who was Vicar of Catterick, part of his reward for his work for Nelson. Alfred and Margaret Gatty were married in 1839 and immediately moved to Ecclesfield where Alfred had been appointed vicar, a post that he occupied for nearly sixty-four years until his death in 1903 at the age of eighty-nine. Alfred Gatty led a very active life. Not only was he vicar of an enormous parish (which was gradually reduced in size as the century wore on); he modernised and beautified St Mary's church at Ecclesfield; he and his family socialised with the local aristocracy (the 6th Earl Fitzwilliam (1815–1902) had been his fag at Eton!) and local professional and industrial families, e.g., lawyers such as the Bingleys of Whitley Hall and the Hindes of Bradfield, Bernard Wake, Dr Aveling, and the silversmiths, the Dixons, of Page Hall and Birley Carr; and he wrote and edited all his life. His best known works are his revised editions (1969 and 1875) of Hunter's *Hallamshire* and his

Alfred Gatty (1813–1903) and Margaret Gatty (1809–1873). Alex and Joan Swann

popular (and it may be said well researched and very readable) history of Sheffield, *Sheffield Past and Present* (1873). Among his other publications were four published volumes of sermons, a book about the bell (not just church bells but also about other bells such as the school bell and the muffin bell), a book on the poetry of Lord Tennyson (who was a family friend) and a substantial number of sermons and the texts of lectures he had given.

But he was far outshone in the literary sphere by his wife, Margaret. In between giving birth to and bringing up ten children (eight of whom survived to adulthood) she wrote and had published a number of best-selling children's books including three series of *Parables from Nature* (1855–71), thirty-seven parables altogether, 'to gather moral lessons from some of the wonderful facts of God's creation', such things as the migratory urge of the sedge warbler, the purring of cats and the chirping of house crickets. One reviewer said of the first series that 'There is more poetry in this little book than in half the poems that come forth'. Even more famously she was the author of *Aunt Judy's Tales* (1859), based on goings-on in the nursery at Ecclesfield vicarage, 'Aunt Judy' being her second-eldest daughter, Juliana. The *Athenaeum* said that 'Aunt Judy is the essence of the excellencies of all the Aunts in Christendom' and predicted that she 'may become the toast and rage in nursery regions'.

Such was her fame that her publisher asked her in 1866 to edit a children's magazine, which she did until her death in 1873. Significantly it was called *Aunt Judy's Magazine*. And she attracted to it some very well-known authors. Translations of stories by Hans Christian Andersen regularly appeared, Lewis Carroll contributed a story, and most of her daughter Juliana's very popular stories appeared for the first time in the magazine. Famous Victorian illustrators also contributed: George Cruikshank, Helen Patterson, Randolph Caldecott and Gordon Browne. The magazine had a world-wide not just a British readership. Mrs Gatty also pulled off a remarkable charitable coup through the magazine's pages. In 1868 after being prompted by the hospital's secretary she suggested to her readers that they may wish to contribute financially ('every contribution, however trifling, will be acknowledged') to the funding of children's beds at Great Ormond Street Children's Hospital in London. This led to the sponsorship of the first children's hospital beds anywhere in the world. By 1871 £1,000 had been raised and a girls' cot was permanently established, followed five years later by a boys' cot. And from 1877 the magazine's readers (the magazine was edited by Mrs Gatty's third daughter, Horatia, after her death) from St Petersburg maintained another cot on an annual basis.

But Mrs Gatty's interests went far beyond writing and editing publications for children. In the year before she died she completed with the help of her daughter Horatia (Mrs Gatty by this time was paralysed in both arms, both legs and had lost the power of speech) *The Book of Emblems* and *The Book of Sundials*. But her greatest triumph had come a decade earlier. Margaret Gatty was a consummate naturalist and 1863 saw the publication of her magnificent and very influential *British Seaweeds,* the culmination of fifteen years of obsessive collecting and classifying. The beautifully illustrated book which has been called 'a fool-proof key to British seaweeds' was still in use at marine research stations around the British coast until well into the twentieth century. Mrs Gatty corresponded for years with the main authorities on the subject and had an Australian seaweed *Gattya pinella* and a marine worm *Gattia spectabilis* named after her!

Mrs Gatty was in her turn surpassed as a children's writer by her second daughter, Juliana. She wrote more than a hundred children's stories, most of them published for the first time, before appearing in book form, in *Aunt Judy's Magazine*. She published her first story when she was only nineteen. She was educated at home by her mother

and as a growing girl she organised activities in the nursery at the vicarage, and took a strong role in the education of her brothers and sisters (three of the four boys went to university and two of them were knighted). She also organised a village library and was an assiduous parish visitor sometimes working until she dropped from exhaustion.

In 1867 when she was twenty-five she married a soldier, Captain (and eventually Colonel) Alexander Ewing, and the couple left immediately after their wedding for Canada where

Juliana Horatia Ewing (1841–1885).
From a portrait by George Reid, RSA.

Ewing was stationed for two years. They were billeted in Frederickton, New Brunswick and Juliana wrote regularly from her new army home to her family back in Ecclesfield describing the country and the people and enclosing drawings and water-colour paintings. These letters and many of the drawings have survived.[12] More than one hundred of her illustrated letters have been published in *Canada Home* by Margaret Howard Blom and Thomas E Blom and many of her Canadian drawings and water-colours have appeared in Donna McDonald's *Julina Ewing's Canadian Pictures 1867–1869*.[13] After returning to England the couple lived successively in Aldershot, Bowden in Cheshire and York until 1879 when Alexander Ewing was posted to Malta and then to Ceylon. Juliana tried to join him but fell ill in Paris on the way to Malta and had to be escorted home. The couple were then separated for most of the period between 1879 and 1883 when Alexander returned to England and was stationed at Taunton. Juliana who had been ill for some time died of cancer in 1885 at the young age of forty-three.

Her output in the twenty-four year period from the publication of her first story in 1861 to her premature death in 1885 was prodigious: light verse, lyrics for songs, plays, short stories and full length novels, all for children. Her stories may be divided into three main categories, stories with a local South Yorkshire setting, fairy tales, and a broad miscellaneous category which includes settings and themes based on her life as an army wife. Among the fairy stories *Lob Lie-by-the-Fire* and *The Brownies* are the best known – Baden Powell taking the name 'Brownies' from the latter for the junior branch of the Girl Guides. In the miscellaneous category, *Jackanapes*, the story of a village boy who rescues his village friend in battle but is fatally wounded in the process, is perhaps her best-known story of all. What is particularly interesting is the way Juliana used the love of her local patch: the church and vicarage at Ecclesfield, the local countryside, the local people and the local dialect in a number of her most interesting stories.[14] *Melchior's Dream,* for instance, her first published story, is a moving Christmas tale set in a northern vicarage just like the one at Ecclesfield, and in *The Yew-Lane Ghosts* she uses a real Ecclesfield street name. Perhaps the best-known and best loved of her stories with a local setting is *Daddy Darwin's Dovecot* written in 1881. It is the story of a workhouse orphan (there was a workhouse at Grenoside and Juliana used to invite the children from there for tea and games at the vicarage on her birthday), about his adoption by an old man who keeps pigeons, about the theft of the pigeons and their recovery, about the growing relationship between the boy and the old man and about the love of the boy for his neighbour's daughter. The story is firmly set in the Ecclesfield countryside, peopled by Ecclesfield types, speaking the local dialect.

Although largely forgotten now, Juliana Ewing's books sold in their thousands and in her lifetime she was compared to Lewis Carroll and Robert Louis Stevenson and was much admired by John Ruskin. Early in the last century Rudyard Kipling and Arnold Bennett extolled her virtues as a writer.

Equally lost from the memories of most present-day Sheffielders is **James Montgomery** (1771–1854). He was a Scot and his father was pastor of the Moravian church in Irvine in Ayrshire and when he was six Montgomery was sent to the Moravian school at Fulneck near Leeds. While he was at school in Leeds his parents went as missionaries to the West Indies and they died there. Meanwhile the school authorities apprenticed Montgomery – who was sixteen and already writing poetry – to a baker in Mirfield but he hated the employment and ran away and turned up in Wath where he found employment in a general store. Before long he left and went to London, worked for a publisher and bookseller, and hoped to find a publisher for his poems. Failing miserably in this endeavour, after less than a year he returned to his job in Wath where one day, in 1792 when he was just twenty, he saw an advertisement in the *Sheffield Register* for a clerk on the newspaper. Montgomery applied and secured the post.

The owner and editor of the *Sheffield Register*, Joseph Gales, was an outspoken radical who supported the French Revolution – he had roasted an ox in celebration of the success of 'our French brethren over despots and despotism'[15] - and under threat of prosecution by the government fled to the United States, leaving Montgomery in charge, not now just a clerk and journalist, but editor and eventually proprietor. But within a year his inexperience got him in trouble with the authorities. He published on the newspaper's presses a ballad which was deemed to contain seditious sentiments ('… should France be subdued, Europe's liberty ends, If she triumphs the world will be free.') and he was tried at Doncaster quarter sessions in January 1795, fined £20 and imprisoned for three months in York Castle. Within a year of his release he was in prison again at York Castle, this time for six months for libel following his highly critical report on Colonel Althorpe's leadership of the Volunteer Militia when they dispersed a large crowd that had gathered in Norfolk Street around a group of Volunteer privates who were complaining about their pay being witheld, and shot at and killed two men and wounded several others.

But Montgomery returned to Sheffield and to his newspaper. He had renamed it the *Sheffield Iris* and remained editor for thirty-one years, eventually retiring in 1825. In those thirty-one years he mounted long-term campaigns in its columns against slavery and against the 'the barbarous and abominable practice' of employing

Monument to James Montgomery(1771–1854) in the General Cemetery in the nineteenth century. It was removed to a new site beside the Cathedral in 1971, the bi-centenary of his birth. Illustrated Guide to Sheffield and Neighbourhood, Pawson & Brailsford, 1862

young boys and girls to climb up and clean soot-filled chimneys. He also took the part of workmen who were in dispute with their employers and was a model citizen in other ways including being a founder member of the Sunday School Union. He also looked after Gales' three sisters, one of whom outlived him. He did not marry.

He wrote poetry all his life, all of it now forgotten.[16] The early verse written shortly after he came to Sheffield was of a political nature, railing against government corruption and the failure of the Established Church to minister to the working-class population. His longer poems such as 'The Wanderer of Switzerland', 'The West Indies' (celebrating the abolition of slavery) and 'The Pelican Island' came out in several editions and were widely read in this country and abroad. When the poet laureate Robert Southey, died in 1843, Montgomery's name was mentioned in the same breath as William Wordsworth as a possible successor. He was rewarded in 1836 for his services to poetry when Prime Minister Robert Peel placed him on the Civil List with a pension of £200 per year. In the same year William Wordsworth sent Montgomery a new edition of his collected poems, the dedication beginning 'In admiration of genius...'[17].

He was also a prolific hymn writer, ('the Christian poet') of 355 hymns in all. Some of these still appear in modern hymn books, the best known being the carol 'Angels from the Realms of Glory' which made its first appearance in the *Sheffield Iris* on Christmas Eve in 1810.

His funeral was one of the finest that Sheffield has ever known. One hundred and sixty carriages led the procession ahead of the hearse from his home at The Mount in Broomhill to the general cemetery and crowds six deep lined the route. John Newton Mappin, one of Sheffield's leading industrialists, paid for a statue to be raised in his memory. This stood in Sheffield Cemetery until its removal on the bicentenary of his birth in 1971 to a new site outside Sheffield Cathedral. The Montgomery Hall is also named in his memory.

Architects, artists and musicians
Two architectural firms dominated nineteenth century Sheffield: Hadfields and Flocktons. **Matthew Hadfield** (1812–1885) designed a number of Sheffield churches including St John's on Park Hill and St Marie's RC Cathedral (with J G Weightman) and the Royal Victoria Hotel. With his partners he was also responsible for the Norfolk and Fitzalan Market Halls (now demolished).

William Flockton (b. 1804) was the son of a Sheffield carpenter and builder who designed a substantial number of fine buildings which still adorn the townscape including Wesley College (now King Edward

Wesley College, now King Edward VII School, one of the public buildings designed by William Flockton (b.1894). Sheffield and Neighbourhood, Pawson & Brailsford, 1889

VII School) and Ecclesall Union Workhouse (later part of Nether Edge Hospital) and The Mount in Broomhill. Wesley College was described by Sir Nicholas Pevesner as 'a quite exceptionally ambitious piece of school design for its date'.[18] With his partners – his son **Thomas Flockton** and Edward Lee, he was also responsible for a number of churches including Christ Church, Pitsmoor and the New Chapel in the General Cemetery, and Kenwood, the private house of George Wostenholm. After Edward Lee left the firm, it continued as Flockton & Son and they continued to design important houses for leading manufacturers including Tapton Hall for Edward Vickers, Oakbrook for Mark Firth and Endcliffe Hall for Sir John Brown.

Sheffield can claim a slight or fleeting association with a number of important Victorian artists. Dorset-born sculptor **Alfred Stevens** (1817–1875) was employed in Sheffield from 1850–52 as a designer of stove grates and fenders by Hoole, Robson and Hoole at their Green Lane Works. Longer resident in Sheffield was another outsider **Godfrey Sykes** (1825–1866) who was born in Malton in the North

Riding and came to Sheffield as a student at the School of Design (later the School of Art) and was a master there for a few years. He also worked as an engraver and stove grate designer in the town and completed a number of interesting paintings of the local industrial scene. He was also employed as an interior designer by local businessmen and designed the gates to Weston Park. In 1861 he left Sheffield for London for his best-known work before his early death from consumption – the decoration of the Victoria and Albert Museum. Also born and resident in London for most of her life was **Elizabeth (Lizzie) Siddal** (1829–1862), wife of Dante Gabriel Rossetti, the Pre-Raphaelite painter. At first only recognised as muse of the Pre-Raphaelites and model for many of their most famous paintings she is now increasingly recognised as a talented artist in her own right, her promise cut short by her early death from an overdose of laudanum.[19] The Sheffield connections are two-fold: her father Charles Siddall (the original spelling of the family name) was a Sheffield-born cutler who had a wholesale and retail cutlery business in London and in the summer of 1857 Lizzie came on a long visit to Sheffield where she stayed with relatives and attended classes at the School of Art. While in Sheffield she met and became friendly with **William Ibbitt** (1804–1869) silversmith, local councillor and self-taught artist. Ibbitt is best known for his engraved panoramic views of Sheffield, for example, his well-known 'South East view of Sheffield' (1854) and less well-known semi-rural 'North West view of Sheffield from Parkwood Spring' (*c.* 1850) and 'Valleys of the Sheaf'(1857).

The most famous local artist of the nineteenth century was **Sir Francis Chantrey** (1781–1841) who was born in Jordanthorpe in Norton parish (then part of Derbyshire), the son of a carpenter and small farmer who rented forty-five acres. He was educated, irregularly, at the village school and was a milk-boy going regularly into Sheffield with his donkey, Jock, to deliver milk, butter and eggs before returning with his mother's shopping. He is said to have shown artistic talents at an early age, making drawings on the flags of the kitchen floor of his family's cottage and carving heads on sticks.

He was apprenticed 'on trial' to Ebenezer Birks, a grocer in Fargate in Sheffield but was soon attracted by the nearby shop window of Robert Ramsay, a carver and gilder (who also dealt in prints and plaster-cast models) and Chantrey persuaded his parents to let him be apprenticed to the carver instead of the grocer. He sketched in pencil and then painted in oils. By 1802 he managed to be released from his apprenticeship and set up as a portrait painter. He is known

Sir Francis Chantrey (1781–1841).
Inset: *the Chantrey obelisk in Norton village.* Sheffield and Neighbourhood, Pawson & Brailsford, 1889

to have executed seventy-four portraits before he left Sheffield.

By 1804 he had moved to London and was carving in wood as well as continuing to paint portraits. He soon gave these up to concentrate on sculpture and his first work in marble was of the Revd James Wilkinson of Sheffield for the parish church. From then on he quickly gained recognition and wealth (helped on the way by marrying his cousin who brought him property valued at £10,000). He became the 'chosen sculptor of monarchs and statesmen'[20] and was charging £150 for a bust in 1813 and 200 guineas in 1822. In the same year King George IV paid Chantrey 300 guineas for his bust. He later chiselled busts of the great and good in every walk of life including the novelist Sir Walter Scott and the engineer James Watt and executed important statues including Wellington for the Royal Exchange, William Pitt for Hanover Square and King George IV for Trafalgar Square. His most celebrated work is 'The Sleeping Children' in Lichfield Cathedral.

He was elected a member of the Royal Academy in 1818 and was knighted by William IV in 1835. At his death he was worth £150,000. It was said that his manners were 'somewhat rough and his language strong'. He was an excellent mimic, had a good sense of humour, was a good companion and host, and a keen fisherman and country sportsman. He was well liked by his fellow artists (Turner was an old friend) and generous to his old Sheffield friends and younger members of his profession. He was not ashamed of his humble origins, and rebuilt the family cottage for his mother. He insisted on being buried in Norton churchyard having personally chosen his burial plot there. In the church there is a plaque and a full length plaster cast of Chantrey. In 1854 the so-called 'Chantrey obelisk' was erected on what was left of Norton village green; it is twenty-eight feet high, of granite, and simply inscribed 'Chantrey'.

Three locally-born musicians are also worthy of mention. **Sir William Sterndale Bennett** (1818–1875) was the son of the organist at Sheffield parish church but he left Sheffield before he was four to live with his grandparents in Cambridge. As a seven-year old he became a member of King's College choir and at the age of only ten he was enrolled in the Royal Academy of Music of which institution he became Principal in 1866. He wrote concertos and oratorios. He was knighted in 1871 and has the distinction of being the only Sheffielder who has received a public funeral in Westminster Abbey.

On a lighter note altogether was the musical talent of **Sir Alfred Scott-Gatty** (1847–1918),[21] second son of Dr Alfred Gatty, vicar of Ecclesfield, who became the Garter Principal King of Arms at the College of Arms where he played a leading part in organising the ceremonies connected with the lying in state and funeral of King Edward VII and the coronation of King George V. But Alfred's outside of work activities are perhaps more interesting than his 'day-job'. He was a composer from his youth of popular songs for children and for adults and local carols – he wrote the music for 'A song for the time' and 'Voices from the belfry height', two of the most popular of the Ecclesfield carols still sung today and he published four volumes of popular songs, of which he wrote the music and the words (mostly), some of them cruelly comic, as for example:

Once there lived a little poodle with a coat as white as snow,
And his master lov'd him dearly and his mistress lov'd him so,
That whenever she was eating she gave him the nicest bit,
Till the poodle one fine morning had an apoplectic fit.

In the second verse the poodle gives a little yelp and softly sighs, wags his fluffy little tail and quietly he dies!

Even more astounding was that Alfred was the composer of what used to be called 'Negro Spirituals', or 'Plantation Songs' as he called them in the four volumes of plantation melodies that were published in his name. In a magazine article published in 1904 it was even claimed – quite erroneously – that he had invented the plantation song. He was certainly an early fan of the genre and he gave a concert

A cartoon by 'Spy' of Sir Alfred Scott-Gatty (1847–1918), in his formal costume as Garter King of Arms. Vanity Fair, December, 1904

of 'Christy Minstrell Songs' in Ecclesfield vicarage as early as 1862 when he was fifteen. Later in life while a student at Cambridge and then as a herald at the College of Arms he performed his comic and plantation songs at numerous charity events.

Alfred Scott-Gatty's nephew, **Nicholas Comyn Gatty** (1874–1946), Bradfield-born son of his elder brother Reginald, was also a composer of orchestral works, chamber and piano music, and most significantly of operas.[22] Nicholas and his brother Ivor (who taught art at the City Grammar School in Sheffield for many years) were friends of Ralph Vaughan Williams whom they had met and played music with at Cambridge. Vaughan Williams and his wife Adeline were regular visitors to the vicarage at Hooton Roberts where Reginald had become rector in 1884, and where 'walks, picnics, croquet and rough music' filled their days. Vaughan Williams composed *Linden Lea* in the vicarage garden in 1901 and it received its first public performance in the village in 1902.

8   *E*DWARDIAN SHEFFIELD IN PICTURE POSTCARDS

The picture postcard as we know it today came into existence in January 1902. From that date, what was to become until recent times, the standard-sized card – $5^{1}/_{2}$ inches by $3^{1}/_{2}$ inches – was allowed by the Post Office to have one side entirely devoted to an illustration in the form of a photograph, painting or engraving and the other side divided into two with room for a message on the left and the address on the right.

With as many as five deliveries a day from Monday to Saturday and one on Sunday morning, the cards costing just a penny or two to buy, and a halfpenny to post, and cards posted locally often being delivered on the same day as they were posted, picture postcards became during the Edwardian period (1901–1910), the standard way of communicating between places in the days before most people had a telephone. As a result, photographic firms rushed to fill the booming market for postcards featuring photographs of local places and events.[1]

And people collected them in albums right from the beginning. A postcard in the author's possession of Burncross Cemetery at Chapeltown posted in 1904 has the simple message on the back of the card: 'One for your Collection', and the postcard of Brocco Bank (see page 148) carries the message 'For your Picture Postcard Album'.

Some firms catered for the national market. The most famous of these was Frith's whose archive has survived and contains over a third of a million pictures of 7,000 villages and towns including many of Sheffield and the surrounding area. Other firms from different parts of the country also engaged photographers to produce cards of the Sheffield area - Landscape View Publishers of Market Harborough in Leicestershire, Scott Russell & Co, Art Publishers of Birmingham, A. & G. Taylor of Aldersgate Street in London and the Photochrome Co.Ltd. of London and Tunbridge Wells all published cards of the Sheffield area. Valentine's of Dundee and London, was another well-known national company that produced local cards as was Rafael Tuck & Sons 'Art Publishers to their Majesties the King & Queen'. Boots the Chemists also produced local cards.

But cards were produced much closer to home, and village stores and post offices had their own cards produced. Local photographic firms and wholesale stationers from the towns in the region sent photographers out to record scenes and events. Cards of several local places were produced by J M Bowns, wholesale stationers, who were based on Ecclesall Road in Sheffield, ones of the boating lake in Endcliffe Park were by G Bagshaw and Sons also of Ecclesall Road, and ones of Sheffield parish church were marketed by F Chinn, stationer, of West Bar, Sheffield. There are also postcards of Firth Park produced by Bernard P Hall & Co, Art Publishers, of Bakewell. Two important Sheffield photographic firms that produced interesting picture postcards were both from Langsett Road: Furniss and W R Moore. Even John Walsh Ltd, the department store, published its own cards.

The best-known local photographer producing postcards was Edgar Leonard Scrivens of Doncaster. Scrivens was born in 1883 and worked as a press photographer before starting a photographic business in Doncaster in 1909. Between then and the 1930s he took photographs of all the villages and towns, country houses and major events within a 40–mile radius of Doncaster. As he built up his photographic collection he developed a meticulous cataloguing system. Every card has either his initials 'E.L.S.' or his surname: 'Scrivens' together with a series of numbers. Usually there are two numbers, one being the name of the place (Chapeltown was place 234 and Wentworth 165) and the other the number of the photograph. In the 1920s and 1930s Scrivens re-photographed areas he had taken earlier adding a letter G or V to the number to indicate that it was a second series. Remarkably after he died in 1950, Scrivens' methodically catalogued negatives were not saved, but his postcards have and are eagerly sought after by collectors.

The scenes and events portrayed on the Edwardian postcards of Sheffield were very varied. The town centre appeared on a whole series of cards, there were views of suburban scenes, historic and important recent buildings, parks, gardens and the surrounding countryside, and cards commemorating important or unusual events. Nor was Sheffield's industrial function forgotten, with cards of industrial and smoky Sheffield and Sheffield craftsmen.

The Edwardian picture postcard tells us much about the changing face and social geography of Sheffield in the first decade of the twentieth century including changes in public transport; slum demolition and street widening; new house building in the growing suburbs; new public building, and access to parks and the countryside.

Five cards have been chosen to portray the Edwardian city centre. The first one shows the new Town Hall on the corner of Surrey Street and Pinstone Street where an area of old housing had been demolished to make way for the new structure which was replacing

The new Town Hall built between 1891 and 1897. Author's postcard collection

the old town hall on the corner of Castle Street and Waingate. It was designed by E W Mountford, and built between 1891–96 and opened the following year by Queen Victoria who was greeted by Sheffield's first Lord Mayor, the Duke of Norfolk. The queen's visit, the first to Sheffield by a reigning monarch, was accompanied by a visit to Charles Cammell's Cyclops Steelworks to see armour plate being manufactured 'which guards your Empire upon the sea' as the Corporation address to Her Majesty put it.[2] Photographs taken at the time show Queen Victoria still seated in her horse-drawn carriage in the works watching the spectacular display of a sheet of red hot amour plate going through the rollers accompanied by loud reports and hissing steam as heather and birch were thrown onto the plate to blow the scale off it and prevent it from being rolled in.

Built of Derbyshire sandstone, the new Town Hall was described by Sir Nicholas Pevsner as a 'large picturesque pile'.[3] Reflecting Sheffield's industrial history there are two friezes carved in stone which depict, among other things, grinders, smiths, smelters and miners, and, clearly visible on the postcard, a 200 foot tower surmounted by an eight-feet high bronze statue of Vulcan, the Roman god of fire and furnaces, with his right foot on an anvil, a hammer in his right hand and pincers in his left hand.

The second card shows a busy street scene with many pedestrians, a cyclist, two horse drawn cabs and three electric trams at Moorhead,

Moor Head, Sheffield.

Moorhead looking along Pinstone Street with St Paul's church in the background on the right. Author's postcard collection

looking north-eastwards along Pinstone Street towards the new Town Hall which is just out of sight. The tall building with the domed clock tower in the central far distance is St Paul's church, designed by members of the Platt family, the Rotherham architects and masons. The building of the church commenced in 1720 but it did not open – as a chapel of ease for the parish church – until 1740. This was because of an argument between the donor of £1,000 for its construction, John Downes, a goldsmith, and the church authorities, about the right of presentation. The dome was paid for by public subscription and added in 1769. The church was demolished in 1938 and the site is now occupied by the Peace Gardens. In the left foreground the large building is the department store of T and J Roberts which had been built in 1882. It was destroyed by German bombs on the first night of the Blitz on Thursday 12 December 1940. The building on the left with the tower, beyond Roberts Brothers Store, is the Salvation Army Citadel and Hostel, opened in 1894. In the right foreground is the Crimean War monument surmounted by a statue of Queen Victoria which was later taken down and the top and bottom sections re-located in the Botanical Gardens. The photograph can be dated fairly precisely because of the open-topped electric trams. The tramway had been taken over by the City Council in 1896, the first electric trams ran in 1899, electrification was completed in 1902, and open-topped trams made their last appearance in 1911.

The third city centre postcard shows the west side of Leopold Street in about 1910. This was a new late Victorian street created by clearing a route between the western end of Fargate in the south and the western end of Church Street in the north. It was one of a number of street improvement schemes approved by the Town Council in 1873. It was named after Prince Leopold, Queen Victoria's youngest son, who in 1879 was on an official visit to open Firth College, forerunner of the University of Sheffield (see below), the new building for the college being the square stone building standing at the far end of the street, designed by Thomas Flockton (see Chapter 7) and E R Robson, the architect to the London School Board. The building, which still stands, was for many years the City of Sheffield's Education Offices, and had its main entrance at the corner of Leopold Street and West Street, and surrounding the doorway are stone carvings representing science and art. Between Firth College and the Grand Hotel can be seen what in Edwardian period were the Boys' Central Schools. The Central Higher School (opened in 1880), as the Central Schools were first called, was the first of its kind in the country. It became fully secondary in 1906 and was divided into boys and girls' schools (occupying the former Firth College building).

The west side of Leopold Street in about 1910. Author's postcard collection

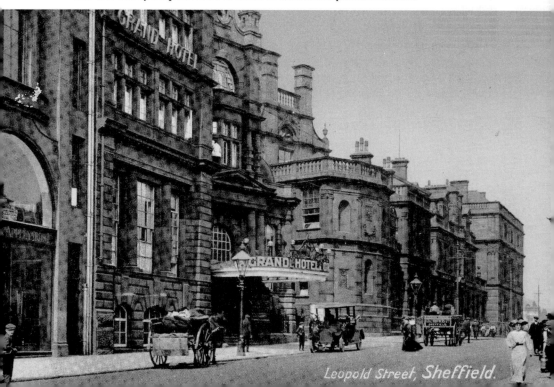

Leopold Street, Sheffield.

The postcard shows the main commercial aspect of the street, the Grand Hotel, now demolished. When the hotel was opened in 1910 a newspaper report had as its headline 'New Centre of Social Life'. The reporter commented that it was somewhat surprising that the city had had to wait so long for 'central hotel facilities as are provided by other places'. Such was the interest and excitement that on the evening of the day of its opening the directors of the hotel entertained about 1,000 prominent local people. They would have been impressed with the splendour of the facilities and decoration. The main lounge was overlooked by a balcony where orchestral music was performed, the dining room accommodated 300 diners and it was the only hotel in the city to have an American bar. No doubt many of the visitors were shown one of the self-contained suites (there was one on each of three floors) each one containing two bedrooms, a sitting room, bathroom and lavatory.[4] It will be noticed that when the photograph was taken Leopold Street was not yet on a tram route, and standing outside the gas-lit main entrance is an early motor car, possibly an early motorised taxi cab. Nearest the camera is the shop of Johnson & Appleyard, cabinet manufacturers.

The fourth city centre postcard shows Fitzalan Square looking northwards towards Haymarket. The tram is waiting at its terminus. The square, as is clearly shown, was also an important place to take

Fitzalan Square looking northwards towards Haymarket. Author's postcard collection

Old timber-framed buildings in Snig Hill. Author's postcard collection

a cab and the structure in the middle of the square was the cab-stand. The building in the background behind the cab-stand is the Fitzalan Market Hall. In the right background at the top of the far side of Commercial Street is the Post Office and on the near side with the classical columns and the tall dome is the offices of the Birmingham, Dudley and District Banking Company (later District and finally Barclays Bank) which was demolished in 1969. Beside that is 'Wonderland' a small theatre on the site of the city's second purpose-built cinema, the Electra Palace (opened in 1911).[5] Wonderland also saw some of the earliest film shows in the city organised (and produced in some cases) by cinema pioneer Jasper Redfern.

The final city centre postcard shows a quite different scene. This shows old buildings in Snig Hill, at least some of them timber-framed as shown by the overlapping upper storeys (jettying). They were demolished in 1900, the street was widened and it became a tram route in 1904. One of Sheffield's earliest public housing schemes replaced the old buildings.

Moving outside of the city centre the next two postcards show quite different scenes. The first one shows the respectable lower-middle class terraces at the entrance to Rossington Road, Newington Road and Wiseton Road at the bottom of Brocco Bank. The iron railings on the right form the fence to the grounds of the George Woofinden Almshouses. Apart from the presence of horse-drawn carts, and the absence of queuing motor traffic, this is a scene not

The bottom of Brocco Bank. Author's postcard collection

Station Road, Chapeltown. Chapeltown & High Green Archive

much changed today. Of a quite different character is the street scene shown in the next postcard, which dates from just after the end of the Edwardian period. It shows Station Road in Chapeltown, then still outside the city limits in the old West Riding. The photograph, which is by Scrivens (E.L.S. 234–18), shows a busy commercial street with an early motor car (a three-wheel Morgan) and the recently built Picture Palace (it was opened in 1912) with an advert for the current film 'Neath the Lion's Paw'. Station Road, formerly called Furnace Lane, was by then the busiest commercial street in this industrial community. Besides the cinema it contained four public houses, branches of the Barnsley British Co-operative Society (grocers, tailors and bootmakers) and the Sheffield & Hallamshire Bank, and various other retail outlets including, a greengrocer, three butchers, a clog and boot dealer, two hairdressers, a stationer and newsagent (who also doubled as a cycle agent), a watchmaker and jeweller, pawnbroker, draper and fishmonger.

Sheffield's small number of historic or modern public buildings also appeared on Edwardian picture postcards. Beauchief Abbey, the Turret House at the Manor Lodge, Bishops' House and the parish church all appeared on a variety of cards as did the medieval parish churches in the surrounding countryside such as Bradfield and Ecclesfield. The postcard of the parish church (it became the cathedral in 1914) – the copy shown here was posted to an address in Gainsborough in Lincolnshire on Christmas Eve 1902 – shows the churchyard still surrounded by a wrought iron fence on which is tied a sign advertising a bible class for men. What the card does show is that history does indeed repeat itself for the overhead wires and tracks for the recently electrified tram system have reappeared in exactly the same spot and the horse cab stand has been replaced by a supertram stop.

Among the few modern buildings that appeared on cards, we have already seen the new Town Hall and this was accompanied by cards

The parish church before it became the Cathedral in 1914. Author's postcard collection

The new red-brick Tudor-style buildings of Sheffield's new university opened by King Edward VII on 12 July, 1905. Author's postcard collection

showing the new university buildings at Western Bank which had been officially opened by King Edward VII on 12 July 1905. The new university, started life as a university college in 1897, being an amalgamation of Firth College (which became the School of Arts and Science), the Medical Institution (which became the Medical School) and the Technical School (which became the School of Technology). A full university charter was granted in 1905, the same year as the new university buildings were opened. The commitment to gain full university status had been spurred on when it was mooted that the University College of Leeds should become the University of Yorkshire.[6] The new red-brick university buildings, (shown here on a card that was posted in 1906) were designed by E Mitchel Gibbs in the Tudor style.

The postcard of the illuminated tramcar is one of a series of postcards printed to coincide with King Edward's and Queen Alexandra's visit to the city to open the new university in 1905. Events of this kind, and of a more local significance were widely recorded on picture postcards. For example, before the introduction of the National Health Service in 1947, hospitals depended for a substantial amount of their money on bequests, endowments and

public generosity. Much money was raised throughout the region from hospital parades. The villagers of Ecclesfield mounted a hospital parade from the 1890s till the 1930s. The custom involved constructing and decorating colourful floats, parading them around the district and with the aid of collectors in fancy dress collecting donations from the crowds that lined the route. On the Saturday afternoon of the third weekend after Whitsuntide the parade left Station Road in the village, went along the Common, up Church Street and via Wadsley Bridge went along Infirmary Road to the bottom of the Moor and then up the Moor along Fargate and High Street to the Wicker, then up to Firth Park and on up Bellhouse Road and back to Ecclesfield. By then it would be late evening and those with the energy went 't'feeast' beside the Ball Inn. W R Moore of Langsett Road seems to have made a special study of the Ecclesfield Hospital Parade in the Edwardian period and a whole series of black and white picture postcards were published of the various floats and collectors. The float shown here outside Ecclesfield church has a mother elephant and her baby. Other contemporary floats featured enormous windmills, royal coaches and a gigantic swan with her family of cygnets (little girls dressed up) on its back. As time went on

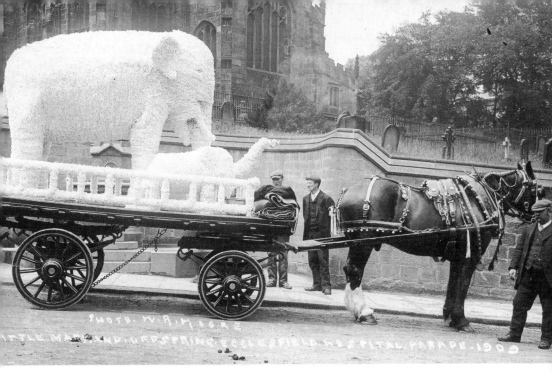

Ecclesfield Hospital Parade float outside St Mary's church, Ecclesfield in 1909.
Author's postcard collection

Ecclesfield Hospital Parade collectors in 1908. Author's postcard collection

Stepping Stones, Endcliffe Woods,
Sheffield.

Charles E. Fl

Stepping stones over the Porter Brook in Endcliffe Woods, on a card posted in 1907.
Author's postcard collection

Boating lake on Holme Wheel dam, Endcliffe Woods, on a card posted in 1905.
Author's postcard collection

BOATING DAM, ENDCLIFFE WOODS, SHEF

more modern subjects such as cameras and aeroplanes appeared. The costumed collectors were no less interesting a sight as the second Ecclesfield Hospital Parade postcard, dated 1908, shows. A variety of headgear and fancy costume was matched by blacked-up and masked faces and a variety of musical instruments.

Postcards with pictures of parks and the surrounding countryside were very popular with visitors to Sheffield. The two park postcards show two very different scenes in what were described as Endcliffe Woods, ie, Endcliffe Park, which was acquired by the Town Council in the 1880s. The first one is an 'Oilette' card by Rafael Tuck & Sons. Cards in this series, painted by Charles F Flower, were made to look like oil paintings but were based on photographs. The stepping stones over the Porter Brook, with Endcliffe Wood in the background, were the subject of numerous picture postcards by a whole host of firms. Even without the date-stamped King Edward VII halfpenny stamp on the reverse of the card used here (2 January 1907), the boy on the stepping stones in his sailor suit leaves no doubt that we are in Edwardian England. The second card shows that the parkland along the Porter valley had had an earlier industrial function that had been converted to recreational use by Edwardian times. The boating lake shown was the dam to Holme Wheel, the mill building, by then used to store gardener's tools, being seen in the background. The first surviving record of Holme Wheel dates from the 1720s when it was leased by the Duke of Norfolk to a cutler, Isaac Staniforth of Little Sheffield. It was rebuilt at least once and operated until about 1890. The dam was in use as a boating lake by 1903.[7] The 'babbling brook' card shows the much more natural countryside of Wyming Brook in the Rivelin valley published by the

Wyming Brook in the Rivelin valley on a card posted in 1906. Author's postcard collection

Birmingham firm of Scott Russell & Co and posted in August 1906, one of a series showing the surviving countryside to the west of the city.

Postcards of scenes of Sheffield's industries were also produced in large numbers. Some of these recorded the traditional skills, settings and products as in the very attractive card of pen-knife grinders. Others recorded the pervading gloom and smoke of an industrial city. The industrial scene portrayed here entitled 'Early Morning on the Don, Sheffield' is another in Rafael Tuck & Sons' 'Oilette' series under the general title 'WORK-A-DAY SHEFFIELD' published just after the end of the Edwardian period. On the back of the card it says

As the sun in the early morning forces its way through the smoke and heat of a thousand furnace fires some beautiful effects can be seen on the murky River Don, which flows right through the busiest part of the town.

Pen-knife grinders. Author's postcard collection

'Early morning on the Don, Sheffield' one of a series of cards produced by Rafael Tuck & Sons under the title 'Work-a-day Sheffield'. Author's postcard collection.

9 𝒫OSTSCRIPT: THE SHAPING OF THE MODERN CITY

Nineteenth century legacy

Looking at the twenty-five inches to one mile Ordnance Survey map of central Sheffield published in 1921 (Yorkshire Sheet 294.8)[1] what strikes the observer is that at the beginning of the third decade of the twentieth century it was still essentially a nineteenth century city. The city centre then contained a substantial number of nineteenth century (or earlier) important buildings that have since been demolished: including the Norfolk Market Hall, Fitzalan Market Hall, the Corn Exchange, the Grand Hotel, St Paul's Church, the Theatre Royal, the Albert Hall, the Hippodrome and the Empire. By 1921 there was hardly an open space to be seen except for the graveyards around the Cathedral and St Paul's. The Ponds area from Shude Hill in the north to the Midland Station in the south, now containing the Ponds Forge Swimming Pool, the Transport Interchange and Sheffield Hallam University, was at the beginning of the 1920s still an industrial area containing a working

Tightly packed streets of small terraced houses, many of them back-to-backs, in the Park Hill area in 1921. Ordnance Survey map of central Sheffield, Yorkshire Sheet 294.08,1921

Ponds Forge, Ponds Steel Works, Soho Rolling Mills, Sheaf Saw Mills, a power station, and various medium-sized and small cutlery works, and with the industrial skyline dotted with travelling cranes and chimney stacks. There was also still a small resident population living on Pond Street and on two lanes off Pond Hill. And beyond the Midland Station to the west on Park Hill, and south as far as Heeley, a warren of brick terrace houses, many of them back-to-backs, clothed the hillside and valley floor.

And beyond the immediate city centre the scene was quite different from that of today. To the west of Lady's Bridge following the River Don upstream there was still a tight cluster of busy small and medium-sized works closely following the banks of the river to Neepsend and beyond surrounded to the north in Burngreave and to the south in Upperthorpe and Crookesmoor by street after street of terrace houses, again many of them back-to-backs. It has been estimated that 17,000 families still lived in back-to-backs in 1914.[2] And of course following the River Don downstream through Brightside, Attercliffe and Darnall to Tinsley almost the whole valley floor was a mass of steel and engineering works surrounded again by tightly packed terrace housing.

To the west and south-west of the city centre the middle class suburbs of Ranmoor, Endcliffe, Ecclesall and Nether Edge were already in place and were to expand rapidly in the inter-war and post-war years. But beyond the areas so far mentioned there were still large stretches and smaller pockets of farmland before the still separate villages of Norton (incorporated into the city in 1901), Handsworth

Smoky Sheffield in the 1920s. Stanley Ellam

(incorporated in 1920) and Stannington (incorporated gradually between 1901 and 1914) were reached. Dore and Totley were still part of Derbyshire and were not incorporated into the city until between 1929 and 1934 and Bradfield, Stocksbridge, Oughtibridge, Worrall, Grenoside, High Green, Chapeltown, Ecclesfield village, Gleadless and Mosbrough would not become part of the city for more than half a century.

But the city began to change dramatically in the 1920s and 1930s, and although development came to a dramatic halt during the Second World War, post-war change was rapid and sustained, and accelerated from the 1970s with the rapid decline of the staple light and heavy steel industries. Gone now are most of the chimneys and the soot and smoke and - most unfortunately - tens of thousands of jobs in manufacturing. It seems staggering that as recently as 1968 a report in the *Guardian* newspaper could describe the streets of Brightside as 'canyons of engineers' brick, broken only by numbered gates and fleeting glimpses of hard graft' with the whole area, houses as well as steelworks, looking 'streaked with dust and sweat'.[3] Now most of the brick canyons have gone, there is very much less dust and little sweat.

Adjusting to change

Sheffield has always been at a locational disadvantage, seen by outsiders as situated in a cul-de-sac on the lower slopes of the Pennines, distant from centres of power and influence. Even as early as 1606 this was an accepted fact in government circles in London. In that year Lord Lisle wrote to Gilbert, 7th Earl of Shrewsbury, hoping he had arrived back safely in Sheffield – 'Halfway to the North Pole'. And this was not improved in the canal age, the canal being opened at its terminus at the Canal Basin in 1819 only six years before the opening of the country's and the world's first railway service between Stockton and Darlington to carry freight and passengers. And when the emerging railway network arrived in the area in 1838 Sheffield found itself on a branch line from Rotherham and was not on a direct line to London till 1870. The twentieth century has also brought mixed fortunes. The railway service to London is poor compared with the east coast line from Doncaster and the much heralded Sheffield Airport has not met with any success. But there have been two relatively successful transport developments, one mostly external and one internal. The external one is of course the M1 motorway and the internal one the supertram system, both contributing to the phenomenal success of Meadowhall Shopping Centre, on the site of Hadfield's East Hecla Works by the Tinsley Viaduct, which has acted as a magnet to entice further development along the Lower Don corridor, but at the same time leading to the stagnation of Sheffield city centre.

The city has continued to evolve during the second half of the twentieth century: much improved housing has spread ever outwards and in a substantial number of cases, upwards; the nineteenth century slums have been cleared (giving way unfortunately in so many cases to twentieth century slums); adjustment to the decline of the staple trades has continued to take place; there have been some notable expansions in non-manufacturing employment; regeneration successes continue to mount up; and much of the glorious countryside surrounding the city and penetrating well into urban areas has been saved. The decline of Sheffield's two staple trades the light steel trades and the heavy steel industry have already been discussed in some detail in Chapters 5 and 6. It is now appropriate to turn attention to two other aspects of Sheffield's recent history that

The Meadowhall Shopping Centre from the air with its parking spaces for 11,000 cars, showing its location almost encircled by a meander of the River Don and adjacent to the Tinsley Viaduct of the M1 motorway. Meadowhall Leisure Shopping

affect residents' lives most closely and which rightly deserve a book to themselves: Sheffield's countryside and housing developments.

Conserving Sheffield's countryside

Even before the Second World War there were dangers from the possible thoughtless transformation of the housing map of the city with unplanned expansion into surrounding farmland and woodland, the still semi-rural river valleys in the south and west, and towards the moorland edge.

Fortunately, Sheffield has always been well served by local conservation societies, none better than the Sheffield, Peak District & South Yorkshire Branch of the Council for the Protection of Rural England (CPRE), which began life in 1924 as the Sheffield Association for the Protection of Local Scenery.[4] It was in 1936 that the Branch turned its attention seriously to the issue of residential expansion into the surrounding countryside – the beautiful frame which held the dirty picture of Sheffield. What started things off was a speculative builder who had purchased eighty-four acres of land on the north side of Hathersage Road between Whirlow Bridge and Long Line and another field south of the Dore Moor Inn and proposed to build 900 houses on the two sites.

In the CPRE's Annual Report for 1936 Ethel Haythornthwaite, who had founded the Branch and was its secretary for fifty-six years, stated that the time had come to 'fix some limit as to where the town should end and the country begin'. The Whirlow proposal, which was eventually rejected, caused the idea of a green belt, then a fairly novel

Sheffield Provisional Green Belt in 1938.

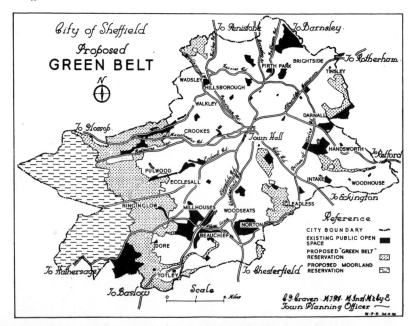

idea, to take hold in the minds of members of the public, and there was mounting pressure to secure such a barrier to wholesale development on all sides of the city where woods and farmland had survived. The breakthrough came in the autumn of 1936 when the Branch was officially invited by the City Council's Town Planning Advisory Committee to submit proposals in the form of a map 'as to areas on all sides of Sheffield which might suitably be preserved as a Green or Agricultural Belt'. The deadline was the middle of January 1937.

The map (submitted on 1 February 1937) identified all those areas that should be included in the green belt, the largest being the areas of moorland and upland pasture in the western parts of the city, dotted with 'stone farms', whose development it was stated, would not only inflict on the citizens of Sheffield an irreparable loss but would also 'injure the city's prestige'. There were also strong recommendations concerning how land in the green belt ought to be treated ('kept strictly rural'), about building materials, about the City Council acquiring land for inclusion in the green belt, and about co-operating with the surrounding local authorities in the West Riding and Derbyshire. *Provisional* green belt proposals by the Planning Committee, based largely on the recommendations of the Sheffield Branch of the CPRE were eventually approved by the City Council on 1 June 1938.

There was great disappointment that the City Council did not establish a permanent green belt in the 1950s as part of its Development Plan as local authorities were invited to do in the Government Circular 50/57. The green belt remained provisional until the approval of South Yorkshire County Council's Structure Plan in late 1979, which included broad provision for a green belt around Sheffield. Then in October 1980, in the face of mounting pressure, the City Council decided to prepare a Green Belt Subject Plan. The plan was approved by the City Council in December 1981 and submitted to South Yorkshire County Council for certification of conformity within the County Structure Plan. The related public inquiry was awaited with great anticipation, although, as was the case with local plans, the inspector had no powers to force a decision on the City Council, he could only make recommendations. The public inquiry lasted from 29 June until 25 July, 1982. The inspector did not accept the House Builders' Federation claim that the green belt had been drawn so tight that it did not give adequate room for residential development. In the eleven instances where developers or landowners had objected to sites being included in the Green Belt the inspector turned down every objection. He summarised his argument as follows:

Looking eastwards from Upper Hurst Farm towards Birley Edge, part of the modern green belt in the north of the city. This area was included in the CPRE's green belt recommendations presented to Sheffield Corporation in 1937. Sixty-five acres of land around Birley Edge were acquired by Aldreman J G Graves and presented to the City of Sheffield in 1941. Joan Jones

The green belt is already tightly drawn and the effect of my recommendations is to make it somewhat tighter.

Foremost among the reasons for having the green belt tightly drawn is the remarkable quality of the landscape on all sides of the city but the east. It is a landscape of bold relief with spurs of high land separating valleys which are often deep and which provide natural deep 'green wedges' into the built-up area. The countryside adjoining fulfils magnificently the function of a green belt to provide open country and outdoor recreation within easy reach of people's homes.

In May 1983 the City Council published its response to the inspector's report. It accepted all of his thirty-four recommendations except for three which it only accepted in part. The Green Belt Plan, only slightly modified from the inspector's recommendations was adopted by the City Council as a statutory local plan on 10 November 1983 and it became operative from 5 December 1983. At last permanent protection had been given to the surviving countryside surrounding Sheffield, one of the city's most unusual and greatest attributes.

Housing and re-housing the population

Public housing developments, following the demolition of inner city slums and on green field developments in the middle and outer suburbs were conspicuous features of changing Sheffield in the twentieth century. The first Council housing was built, in the form of blocks of flats housing a population of 700, in the Crofts area in 1904 following the demolition of a notorious 'warren' of slum housing and this was followed in 1906 by the building of the first houses on what one writer has called Sheffield's first 'workmen's garden suburb'[5] – the 'flower estate' at High Wincobank, popularly so-called because of its street names. At a national housing conference in 1905 the design of the estate and its houses drew generous praise from the leaders of the Garden City movement. By 1919 the estate contained 619 houses. The Housing and Town Planning Act of 1909 helped the Council in its bid to solve the housing problem and a substantial number of new housing schemes were developed accompanied by the replacement of privy middens with flushing toilets and the replacement of stand pipes with indoor tapped water supplies.

The inter-war years saw a continuation of the Council's policy to re-house the working population from the slums of the central and industrial areas following the passing of a series of Acts of Parliament and in 1919 appointed Professor P Abercrombie, the eminent architect and town planner, to prepare a development plan which was published as *Sheffield , a Civic Survey* in 1924 and as *Sheffield and District Regional Planning Scheme* in 1931. Under this scheme Abercrombie proposed the demolition of slum housing in the central area and in industrial areas and the re-housing of the population, involving more than 120,000 people. In the event, between 1919 and 1939, the Council demolished nearly 25,000 slum houses and built nearly 26,000 new ones. The largest council housing estate of the inter-war years was the Manor estate built on land that had formerly been part of the manorial deer park and which had then been enclosed as farmland. The estate, which was begun in 1921, contained 3,600 houses by the outbreak of war in 1939, laid out on Garden City principles.[6]

House building came to a halt in 1939 with the onset of the Second World War, when damage during the blitz of December 1940 – 2,849 houses were totally demolished or so badly damaged they had to be demolished and 2, 990 houses badly damaged but capable of repair – increased the urgency of embarking on large-scale council house building in the post-war years.[7] This the City Council did with gusto and between the early 1950s and the 1970s a succession of bold housing schemes erupted onto the scene and by 1969 of the 186,000 dwellings in the city, 69,000 were Council owned and by the early 1980s the figure had risen to 90,000. The most notable of the inner

Part of the Manor Estate showing its Garden City type layout. Ordnance Survey Six-inch sheet CCXCV SW, 1935 with addition in 1948–49

Burning buildings in High Street during the blitz of 1940. Sheffield City Libraries, Local Studies Library

city Council housing schemes were the Netherthorpe and Burngreave high rise blocks and Park Hill and adjacent Hyde Park (together containing 2,300 dwellings) and Kelvin high rise developments, all replacing demolished tightly packed streets of brick terrace housing. Park Hill and Hyde Park although acclaimed by architects and sociological experts in their early days have also been referred to by other experts as extreme examples of sixties architectural brutalism. They have now been partly demolished and the remainder refurbished. Park Hill is now a Grade II (starred) listed building and a further (£40m) refurbishment is proposed to transform the complex into upmarket apartments, rented flats and small business premises. The Kelvin development, a replica on lower ground of the hillside hugging Park Hill flats, described in a City Council publication of 1969 as 'a further step in the progressive redevelopment of old housing areas on the fringe of the Central Area'[8] proved to be technically flawed and a social disaster and has since been completely demolished. Further from the city centre on green field sites large developments have included the Gleadless Valley, Norfolk Park, Low Edges and Mosborough schemes, all having their own distinctive characteristics: Gleadless Valley with its mixed housing styles fitting into a broken landscape still containing nine ancient woods; Norfolk Park with its lofty high-rise blocks overlooking the Sheaf valley; Low

Post-war housing redevelopment: tower blocks replacing demolished terrace housing in Netherthorpe.

Edges with its separation of pedestrian and motorised traffic and Mosborough, added to the city from North Derbyshire in 1967, designed like a miniature new town for the city's overspill population with its nineteen residential townships increasing the resident population there from 35,000 to 85,000.

While the tide of council house building swept ever outwards, mainly to the north and east of the city centre, the 'scarlet fever' of private red-brick detached and semi-detached houses and bungalows filled the southern, south-western and western suburbs of Beauchief, Dore, Totley, Fulwood, Ranmoor, Endcliffe and Ecclesall. But recently this trend has been reversed and it is estimated that eventually there could be as many as 5,000 new apartment homes in and around the city centre. Among those already occupied or well on their way to full occupation are the prestigious West One and Royal Plaza developments in the fashionable 'Devonshire Quarter' around West Street and upper Devonshire Street. West One consists of 500 apartments with restaurants, cafés and bars underneath; Royal Plaza boasts a 24-hour concierge service, underground parking and a central garden area. Besides the new developments are a number of interesting conversions including the old Barclays Bank in Commercial Street which is being turned into fifty-six apartments, and the Pinstone Chambers Building and the Prudential Assurance Building near the Peace Gardens. Further out from the city centre other interesting conversions include the luxury Ward's Brewery complex, called One Eleven and which includes 132 apartments, the Riverside Exchange beside the Don just off the Wicker with 214 apartments and 250,000 square feet of office space, Dixon's silver plate works at Cornish Place and Beckett's Saw Works off Green Lane.

The twenty-first century city
If Sheffield is to compete with other British and European cities for advanced manufacturing jobs, science-based industries and those in

Mixed housing styles and ancient woods in the Gleadless Valley. Joan Jones

the service industries it must attract outside investors. It cannot rely solely on home-grown employment generators. And to do this it must present itself as a modern city with outstanding cultural amenities – museums, galleries and theatres and concert halls; exceptional shopping and eating opportunities in a thriving and vibrant city centre, top quality housing in every kind of location and style; excellent public transport facilities, an efficient road system, large and thriving universities and colleges and easy access to attractive, well-managed and safe parks, woodlands and countryside.

Some of these features are already in place and a number of prestigious regeneration schemes are on the drawing board or are at an early stage in their development. The Heart of the City scheme has seen the opening of the Millennium Galleries and the Winter Gardens and the re-designing of the Peace Gardens. Riverside developments such as the Riverside Exchange described above and the proposed pedestrianisation of Nursery Street are also notable extensions to the Victoria Quays development at the Canal Basin. The Botanical Gardens have benefited from Heritage Lottery funds as have twenty-three of the city's ancient woods, and the Don Valley Stadium, Arena and Ponds Forge have now been joined by the £12.7m 'iceSheffield'; and the £26m English Institute of Sport. And there is more change on its way. The City Hall is being re-furbished at a cost of over £12m, the money coming mainly from the European Union and central Government, Weston Park Museum and the Mappin Art Gallery are undergoing a nearly £20m Heritage Lottery facelift, a new hotel is rising beside the Winter Gardens, the entry into Sheffield outside the Midland Station (which has itself recently undergone an £11m improvement scheme) is planned to be transformed at a cost of £12.3m by creating a new public plaza out of the present Sheaf Square roundabout with water features and a 90

City living: the West One develoment in the Devonshire Quarter. Joan Jones

metre-long steel sculpture representing a knife blade, and the Leopold Street education department, formerly the Central Schools and Firth College, is about to undergo a £20m transformation into 37 apartments, a 134-bedroom hotel together with a number of restaurants, health club and jazz venue.

Sheffield's lowly position in the league table of provincial shopping centres, eighteenth in the most recent study (December 2003) and far behind regional rivals Manchester (third), Nottingham (fifth) and Leeds (sixth) underlines the problems the city – which is the fourth largest city in the country let us not forget – faces if it is to compete successfully with other centres. That study was based not only on the volume of retail floor space but also on factors such as the quality and quantity of top retail names and the comfort for the shopper in terms of accessibility by public transport, the amount of safe parking and personal safety. It is hoped that the proposed £400m retail quarter between Moorhead, Pinstone Street and Barkers Pool with a new and much larger John Lewis store at its heart and the re-location of the market quarter from Castlegate to the Moor, related to a range of environmental improvements in and around the Moor, will provide the platform for the city centre's retail revival.

Sheffield is certainly a city on the move; it is being shaped and re-shaped by public investment and private enterprise; whether in the right direction and with the most appropriate balance only time will tell.

The Winter Gardens. Joan Jones

Notes and References

Chapter 1
1. A term invented by O Rackham in *Trees and Woodlands in the British Landscape*, J M Dent & Sons Ltd, 1976, p 40.
2. V M Conway, 'Ringinglow Bog, near Sheffield, Part I, Historical', *Journal of Ecology*, 34, 1947, pp 149–181; S P Hicks, 'Pollen-analytical evidence for the effect of pre-historic agriculture on the vegetation of North Derbyshire', *New Phytology*, 70, 1971, pp 647–667.
3. M Dunnin, S Ellis and D Weir, 'The palaeoenvironmental survey of the West Thorne and Hatfield Moors', in E Van de Noort and S Ellis (eds), *Wetland Heritage of the Humberhead Levels*, Humber Wetland Project, University of Hull, 1996, pp 81–156.
4. R Gatty, Chapter X, 'Bradfield' in A Gatty, *A Life at One Living*, Bell & Sons, 1884, p 202.
5. M Jones, *Wincobank Hill: Heritage Site and Vantage Point*, illustrated leaflet, Department of Land & Planning, Sheffield City Council, 1990.
6. P Beswick and D Merrills, 'L H Butcher's Survey of Early Settlements in the Southern Pennines', *Transactions of the Hunter Archaeological Society*, 12, 1983, pp 16–50.
7. I D Latham, *A desk-top assessment of the archaeological potential of the Wharncliffe Forest*, South Yorkshire Archaeological Unit for the South Yorkshire Forest Partnership, 1994.
8. F L Preston, 'A Field Survey of the 'Roman Rig' Dyke in South West Yorkshire, Part 1', *Transactions of the Hunter Archaeological Society*, 6, 1944–50, pp 197–220; F L Preston, 'A Field Survey of the 'Roman Rig' Dyke in South West Yorkshire, Part 2', *Transactions of the Hunter Archaeological Society*, 6, 1944–50, pp 285–309; N Boldrini, 'Creating Space: A Re-examination of the Roman Ridge', *Transactions of the Hunter Archaeological Society*, 20, 1999, pp 24–30.
9. The main general studies of place-names are K Cameron, *English Place-Names*, Batsford, revised edition, 1996; E Ekwall, *The Concise Oxford Dictionary of English Place-Names*, fourth edition, Oxford University Press, 1966; M Gelling, *Signposts to the Past: Place-Names and the History of England*, third edition, Phillimore, 1997. The main local studies are K Cameron, *The Place-Names of Derbyshire, Parts I, II and III*, English Place-Name Society, Volumes XXVII-XXIX, Cambridge University Press; 1954 and A H Smith, *The Place-Names of the West Riding of Yorkshire, Part I, Lower & Upper Strafforth and Staincross Wapentakes*, English Place-Name Society, Volume XXX, Cambridge University Press,1961. Interesting local interpretations of place-names in the landscape include D Hey, *Medieval South Yorkshire*, Chapter 2, 'The Origins of Local Place-Names', Landmark Publishing, 2003, pp 25–38; M Jones, *The Making of the South Yorkshire Landscape*, Chapter 3, 'Place-Names in the Landscape', Wharncliffe Books, 2000, pp 21–30; and I Maxwell, 'The Age of Settlement' in D L Linton (ed), *Sheffield and Its Region*, British Association for the Advancement of Science, 1956, pp 121–137.
10. Cameron, *English Place-Names*, p 31.
11. Gelling, *Signposts to the Past*, Chapter 5, 'The Chronology of English Place-Names', pp 106–129.
12. M Jones, *Sheffield's Woodland Heritage*, third edition, Wildtrack Publishing / Green Tree Publications, 2003, pp 10–11.
13. Smith, *Place-Names of the West Riding of Yorkshire, Part I*, pp 194–195.
14. J G Ronksley, (ed) *An exact and perfect Survey and View of the Manor of Sheffield with other lands by John Harrison, 1637*, Robert White & Co, 1908.
15. M Bragg, *The Adventure of English: the biography of a language*, Chapters 3–5, Hodder & Stoughton, 2003.
16. Cameron, *English Place-Names*, p 94.

Chapter Two
1. A L Armstrong, 'Sheffield Castle', *Transactions of the Hunter Archaeological Society*, IV, 1937, pp 7–27.
2. J G Ronksley (ed), *An exact and perfect Survey and View of the Manor of Sheffield with other lands by John Harrison, 1637*, Robert White & Co., 1908, p 47.
3. D Postles, *Sheffield in 1581*, Sheffield City Libraries, 1981.
4. J R Wigfull, 'House Building in Queen Elizabeth's Days', *Transactions of the Hunter Archaeological Society*, III, 1929, pp 66–73.
5. J D Leader, *Records of the Burgery of Sheffield*, 1897, p 26.
6. J R Wigfull, 'Lady's Bridge, Sheffield', *Transactions of the Hunter Archaeological Society*, I, 1918, pp 57–63.
7. Ronksley, *Survey of the Manor of Sheffield*, pp 43–46.
8. Leader, *Records of the Burgery of Sheffield*, p 43.
9. Ronksley, *Survey of the Manor of Sheffield*, pp 335–336.
10. A H Thomas, 'Some Hallamshire Rolls of the Fifteenth Century' *Transactions of the Hunter Archaeological Society*, II, 1924, p 74.
11. Ronksley, *Survey of the Manor of Sheffield*, p 4.
12. J Evelyn, *Silva or a Discourse of Forest Trees*, 4th edition, 1706, p 229.
13. Ronksley, *Survey of the Manor of Sheffield*, p 152.

14. T W Hall, *A Descriptive Catalogue of Sheffield Manorial Records*, Volume 1, 1926, p 3.
15. T W Hall, *A Descriptive Catalogue of Sheffield Manorial Records*, Volume 2, 1926, p 11.
16. *Catalogue of the Arundel Castle Manuscripts*, Sheffield City Libraries, 1965, Calendar of the Talbot Correspondence, p 201.
17. Thomas, 'Some Hallamshire Rolls', p 157.
18. 'The Court Leet of the Manor of Sheffield' *Transactions of the Hunter Archaeological Society*, III, 1929, p 148.
19. C Drury, 'The Funeral of Francis Talbot, Earl of Shrewsbury at Sheffield, 1560', *The Sheffield Miscellany*, Pt 4, 1897, p 140.
20. M Jones, 'Deer in South Yorkshire: an Historical Perspective', in M Jones, I D Rotherham and A J McCarthy (eds), *Deer or the New Woodlands?, The Journal of Practical Ecology and Conservation*, Special Publication No 1, November 1996, pp 11–26.
21. Ronksley, *Survey of the Manor of Sheffield*, pp 50–55.
22. Evelyn, *Silva*, pp 229–230.
23. University of Nottingham, Tree-ring Dating Laboratory, initial report, January 1992.
24. 'An Inventorie of all the Household Goods and Furniture belonginge to George Earl of Shrewsbury at Sheffield-Castle and the Lodge, 1582', *Journal of the British Archaeological Association*, XXX, p 260.
25. *Catalogue of the Arundel Castle Manuscripts*, Sheffield City Libraries, 1965, Calendar of the Talbot Correspondence, p 204.
26. Ronksley, *Survey of the Manor of Sheffield*, p 48.

Chapter 3

1. Antonia Fraser, *Mary Queen of Scots*, Weidenfeld & Nicholson, 1969.
2. G Donaldson, *Mary, Queen of Scots*, The English Universities Press Ltd, 1974.
3. J Guy, *'My Heart is My Own': The Life of Mary Queen of Scots*, Fourth Estate, 2004.
4. J Hunter, *Hallamshire: The History and Topography of the Parish of Sheffield*, revised by Alfred Gatty, Virtue and Company, 1875.
5. Hunter, *Hallamshire*, p 85.
6. Hunter, *Hallamshire*, pp 85–96.
7. A Gatty, 'The Captivity of Mary, Queen of Scots', *Aunt Judy's Magazine*, Christmas Volume, Bell and Daldy, 1871, pp 434–39.
8. A Gatty, *Sheffield: Past and Present*, Thomas Rodgers (Sheffield) and Bell & Sons (London), 1875, Chapter III, pp 31–72.
9. J D Leader, *Mary Queen of Scots in Captivity: a Narrative of Events*, Leader & Sons (Sheffield) and Bell & Sons (London), 1880.
10. J K Cheetham, *Mary Queen of Scots – The Captive Years*, J. W. Northend Ltd, 1982; and *On the Trail of Mary Queen of Scots*, Luath Press Ltd., 1999.
11. Letter from Sir Francis Knollys 15 June 1568 quoted in Leader, *Mary Queen of Scots in Captivity*, p 7.
12. Letter by Mary quoted in Leader, *Mary Queen of Scots in Captivity*, pp 23–24.
13. 'An Inventorie of all the Household Goods and Furniture belonginge to George Earl of Shrewsbury at Sheffield-Castle and the Lodge, 1582', *Journal of the British Archaeological Association*, XXX, pp 251–263.
14. Letter from Gilbert Talbot quoted in Hunter, *Hallamshire*, p 90.
15. Letter from Lord Burghley (William Cecil), Queen Elizabeth's Secretary of State, to the Earl of Shrewsbury, quoted in Leader, *Mary Queen of Scots in Captivity*, p 90.
16. Letter by Mary quoted in Hunter, *Hallamshire*, p 92.
17. Letter by Mary quoted in Hunter, *Hallamshire*, p 92.
18. Letter by Mary quoted in Leader, *Mary Queen of Scots in Captivity*, p 318.
19. Letter by the Earl of Shrewsbury to Sir Francis Walsingham, Queen Elizabeth's joint Secretary of State, quoted in Leader, *Mary Queen of Scots in Captivity*, p 329.
20. Letter by Mary quoted in Hunter, *Hallamshire*, p 92.
21. Letter by Mary quoted in Hunter, *Hallamshire*, p 92.
22. Letter from the Earl of Shrewsbury, dated 3 March 1575, to Lord Burghley quoted by Hunter, *Hallamshire*, p 92.
23. Letter by Mary, dated 2 March 1575, to the French Ambassador quoted in Leader, *Mary Queen of Scots in Captivity*, p 356.
24. Hunter, *Hallamshire*, p 83.

Chapter 4

1. The most complete source on the cholera epidemic in Sheffield in 1832 is John Stokes, *The History of the Cholera Epidemic of 1832 in Sheffield*, J W Northend, 1921.
2. Quoted by Stokes, *Cholera Epidemic*, p 2.
3. Charles Darwin, *The Voyage of H.M.S Beagle*, Folio Society edition, 2003, p 3.
4. The journal of Joseph Woodcock is still in the hands of his family. I acknowledge the permission given to me by Geoffrey Woodcock to quote freely from the section on the cholera epidemic.

5. Woodcock's Journal, p 100A.
6. Woodcock's Journal, pp 84– 85.
7. *The Builder*, 21 September 1861 and 5 October 1861.
8. Quoted by Stokes, *Cholera Epidemic*, p 16.
9. Quoted by Stokes, *Cholera Epidemic*, pp 123–126.
10. Woodcock's Journal, p 98.
11. Woodcock's Journal, pp 98 and 99 A.

Chapter 5
1. J E Oxley, 'Notes on the History of the Sheffield Cutlery Industry', *Transactions of the Hunter Archaeological Society*, VII, Pt 1, 1953, pp 1–10.
2. W Brown (ed), *Yorkshire Lay Subsidy 25 Edwardi I*, Yorkshire Archaeological Society Record Series, 1894, p 76.
3. *The returns of the Poll Tax for the West Riding of Yorkshire, 1379*, Yorkshire Archaeological and Topographical Society, 5, 1882.
4. L T Smith (ed), *Leland's Itinerary in England and Wales*, 1914, lv, p 14.
5. G I H Lloyd, *The Cutlery Trades: an historical essay in the economics of small-scale production*, 1913, pp 95–96.
6. Lloyd, *The Cutlery Trades*, p 96.
7. K C Barraclough, *Sheffield Steel*, Sheffield City Museums/Moorland Publishing Co Ltd, 1976, p 9; C Binfield and D Hey (eds) *Mesters to Masters: a History of the Company of Cutlers of Hallamshire*, Oxford University Press, 1997, p 15.
8. Borthwick Institute of Historical Research, University of York, Prob. Reg. V8, f551.
9. D Smith, 'John Spencer's Baltic Trade in Sheffield Wares', in M Jones (ed) *Aspects of Sheffield: Discovering Local History, Volume 2*, Wharncliffe Publishing Ltd, 1999, pp 12–13.
10. J G Ronksley, *An exact and perfect Survey and View of the Manor of Sheffield and other lands by John Harrison*, 1637, Robert White & Co, 1908, pp 3 and 31–32.
11. Smith, 'John Spencer's Baltic Trade…,' pp 8–11.
12. J. Richardson, ' Early Sheffield Assay Masters and Assay Offices; in M. Jones (ed) *Aspects of Sheffield: Discovering Local History, Volume 2*, 1999, pp 16–31.
13. Lloyd, *The Cutlery Trades, 1913*, p 179.
14. G Tweedale, *The Sheffield Knife Book*, The Hallamshire Press, 1999, Chapter 3, 'Sheffield and America', pp 27–36.
15. A Gatty, *Sheffield Past and Present*, Thomas Rodgers/Bell & Sons, 1873, p 197.
16. William Nesbitt's diaries are unpublished and in the hands of his family. I acknowledge the permission of Mrs C J Durdy to quote from them.
17. Lloyd, *The Cutlery Trades*, p 187.
18. See, for example, M Jones, 'The World of William Steel: the Diaries of a Birley Carr Filecutter and Lay Preacher', *Transactions of the Hunter Archaeological Society*, 21, 2001, pp 86–111.
19. S Pollard, *A History of Labour in Sheffield*, Liverpool University Press, 1959, pp 206–207.
20. Report of the Chief Inspector of Factories, 1908, quoted by Lloyd, *The Cutlery Trades*, p 182.

Chapter 6
1. S Pollard, *A History of Labour in Sheffield*, Liverpool University Press, 1959.
2. T Lodge, 'Henry Bessemer: Sheffield's Radical Steelmaker' in M Jones (ed) *Aspects of Sheffield: Discovering Local History, Volume 2*, Wharncliffe Publishing Ltd, pp 164–161.
3. A Gatty, *Sheffield Past and Present*, Thomas Rodgers/ Bell & Sons, 1873, pp 308–309.
4. J Bull, 'The Population Geography of Two Contrasting Artisan Districts in Sheffield in 1871', B Ed dissertation, Sheffield City Polytechnic, 1976.
5. W S Porter and A T Watson (eds), *Handbook & Guide to Sheffield*, British Association for the Advancement of Science/ J W Northend, 1910, p 217.
6. Porter and Watson, *Handbook & Guide to Sheffield*, p 217.
7. Pollard, *A History of Labour in Sheffield*, p 269.
8. Pollard, *A History of Labour in Sheffield*, p 269; D Hey, M Olive and M Liddament, *Forging the Valley*, Sheffield Academic Press, 1997, p 82.
9. T Lodge, 'Chronicles of a Titan: Templeborough Steelworks, 1916–1993' in M Jones (ed) *Aspects of Rotherham: Discovering Local History, Volume 2*, Wharncliffe Publishing Ltd, 1996, pp 234–260.
10. *Sheffield at War*, Sheffield Telegraph & Star Ltd 1948, pp 57–80.
11. *Sheffield at War*, p 64.
12. For up to date detailed accounts of the rapid decline of heavy steel making in the Lower Don Valley see Hey, Olive and Liddament, *Forging the Valley* and S Dalton, *Crashing Steel*, Wharncliffe Publishing Ltd, 1999.

Chapter 7
1. V Doe, 'Some Developments in Middle Class Housing in Sheffield 1830–1875' in S Pollard & C Holmes (eds) *Essays in the Economic and Social History of South Yorkshire*, South Yorkshire County Council, 1976, p 179.

2. J Goddard, 'Endcliffe Hall: the Residence of a Gentleman Industrialist'; in M Jones (ed) *Aspects of Sheffield: Discovering Local History, Volume 1*, Wharncliffe Publishing Ltd, 1997, pp 226–244.
3. J Simmons, *The Victorian Railway*, Thames and Hudson, 1991, p 23.
4. For a short biography including a study of the place where Sir John Fowler was educated see J and M Jones, *Whitley Hall: an illustrated history*, Green Tree Publications, 2002.
5. A Gatty, *Sheffield Past and Present*, Thomas Rodgers/Bell & Sons, 1873, p 236.
6. Gatty, *Sheffield Past and Present*, p 237.
7. For an appreciation of the significance of Hunter's work on the local dialect see J D A Widdowson's Introduction (pp 1a-5a) to the 1983 facsimile edition of *The Hallamshire Glossary*, Centre for English Cultural Tradition and Language, University of Sheffield.
8. Gatty, *Sheffield Past and Present*, p 238.
9. For a recent biography of Elliott see K Morris and R Hearne, *Ebenezer Elliott: Corn Law Rhymer & Poet of the Poor*, Rotherwood Press, 2002.
10. For a recent copiously illustrated study of the history of the Gatty family see J and M Jones, *The Remarkable Gatty Family of Ecclesfield*, Green Tree Publications on behalf of Chapeltown & High Green Archive, 2003.
11. A Gatty, *A Life at One Living*, Bell & Sons, 1884, p 20.
12. In Sheffield Archives, Shoreham Street, Sheffield (letters) and the Headquarters Library, Balne Lane, Wakefield (drawings and paintings).
13. M H and T E Blom (eds), *Canada Home: Juliana Horatia Ewing's Fredericton Letters, 1867–1869*, University of British Columbia Press, 1983 and D McDonald, *Illustrated News: Juliana Horatia Ewing's Canadian Pictures, 1867–1869*, New Brunswick Museum / Dundurn Press. 1985.
14. See M Jones, 'Juliana Ewing, Children's Writer and Ecclesfield's Countryside' in M Jones (ed) *Aspects of Sheffield: Discovering Local History, Volume 2*, Wharncliffe Publishing Ltd, 1999, pp 112–130 and M. Jones, 'West Riding Dialect in the Stories of Juliana Ewing, Victorian Children's Writer', *Transactions of the Yorkshire Dialect Society*, Part XCIX, Volume XIX, pp 29–38.
15. J Derry, *The Story of Sheffield*, Sir Isaac Pitman & Sons Ltd, 1915.
16. For a critical appreciation of Montgomery's poetry see G Wiley, *The Poems of James Montgomery (1771–1854)*, The Hallamshire Press, 2000.
17. Quoted in G Wiley *The Poems of James Montgomery*, p 200.
18. N Pevsner, *The Buildings of England: Yorkshire, The West Riding*, Second Edition revised by Enid Radcliffe, Penguin Books, 1967, p 461.
19. J Marsh, *Elizabeth Siddal: Pre-Raphaelite Artist 1829–1868*, Sheffield Arts Department, 1991.
20. H Armitage, *Chantreyland*, Sampson, Low, Marston & Co Ltd, 1910, p 369.
21. See J and M Jones, *The Remarkable Gatty Family of Ecclesfield*, pp 57–62.
22. W J Elliss, 'Famous Music Masters, No 2 Dr Nicholas Comyn Gatty, *What's on in Sheffield & District*, April 1931.

Chapter 8
1. G Godden. *Collecting Picture Postcards*, Phillimore, 1996; C W Hill, *Picture Postcards*, Shire Books.
2. J H Stainton, *The Making of Sheffield*, E Weston & Sons, 1924, pp 224–225.
3. N Pevsner, *The Buildings of England: Yorkshire, The West Riding*, Second Edition revised by Enid Radcliffe, Penguin Books, 1967, p 452.
4. Cuttings Relating to Sheffield, Volume 4, p 58, Sheffield Central Library, Local Studies Department.
5. C Shaw and C Stacey, 'Sheffield's Cinema History', in M Jones (ed) *Aspects of Sheffield: Discovering Local History, Volume 2*, Wharncliffe Publishing Ltd, 1999, pp 182–200.
6. J A Green, 'The University of Sheffield', in W S Porter & A T Watson (eds) *Handbook & Guide to Sheffield*, J W Northend for the British Association, 1910, pp 135–152.
7. D Crossley with J Cass, N Flavell and C Turner (eds), *Water Power on the Sheffield Rivers*, Sheffield Trades Historical Society and University of Sheffield, Division of Continuing Education, 1989, p 78.

Chapter 9
1. Republished in 2004 by Alan Godfrey Maps at a scale of fourteen inches to one mile.
2. S Pollard, *A History of Labour in Sheffield*, Liverpool University Press, 1959, p 188.
3. The *Guardian*, 27 May, 1968.
4. For an illustrated history of the Sheffield, Peak District and South Yorkshire Branch of the CPRE see M Jones, *Protecting the Beautiful Frame*, The Hallamshire Press, 2001.
5. S Pollard, *A History of Labour in Sheffield*, p 186.
6. For a popular account of the early history of the Manor Estate see M Mercer, *A Portrait of the Manor in the 1930s*, Mediac Ltd / Pickard Publishing, n d.
7. For a detailed account of the Sheffield blitz see M Walton and J P Lamb, *Raiders Over Sheffield*, Sheffield City Libraries, 1980.
8. *Sheffield Emerging City*, Sheffield City Council, Town Planning Committee, 1969, p 59.

Index